A Flyfisher's Guide
to the
Teifi Valley

by

Pat O'Reilly

A Flyfisher's Guide to the Teifi Valley

First published in the United Kingdom in 2005 by

First Nature
Swyn Esgair
Drefach Felindre
Llandysul SA44 5XG
Wales, UK
email: **enquiries@first-nature.com**
website: **www.first-nature.com**

ISBN 0-9549554-0-4

Designed and typeset by First Nature

Printed and bound in Wales by
Gomer Press, Llandysul, Ceredigion

Dedication

To the lovely River Teifi, and to the late Artie Jones, secretary of Llandysul Angling Association for nearly forty years, through whose vision and efforts great fishing is now available to many.

Preface

To mark the fiftieth anniversary of the founding of Llandysul Angling Association, I wrote a book entitled *Tribute to the Teifi*. Since its 1998 publication, 1000 copies of that 150-page hardback guide to the River Teifi were sold, and many people have asked when a second edition will be published.

So is this it? Well, not exactly. While the title *Tribute to the Teifi* would be difficult to improve on (and as you will see, I haven't tried very hard!) the contents certainly deserve a major review. One good reason is that new information is now available about the fisheries – and indeed Llandysul Angling Association has also acquired more fishing, which needs to be included. Then there are, inevitably, a few corrections and updates to information that was incomplete or unavailable when I was writing in 1997.

But by far the most valuable source of guidance on what really needs to be included in this new book about gamefishing in the Teifi Valley has come from people who come here for the fishing. In particular, what they have said they particularly value is the fishery information – the beat maps, access guides, pictures and descriptions of each beat – and advice on tackle, tactics and techniques that increase the chances of success.

Teifi fish are wild, and wild fish are not so easily caught. I do hope that the fishery descriptions and the fishing information will help make your visits to the Teifi more enjoyable and productive.

There was one other message that came back loud and clear from readers of *Tribute to the Teifi*, and it was a request to retain the strong link between enjoyment of fishing and appreciation of the scenic beauty and wildlife diversity of the Teifi Valley. That is a request that I am delighted to do what I can to respond to, and I hope that readers of this new book will enjoy the wildlife and ecology pictures and find the information useful.

After nearly 18 years in the role, at the end of 2004 I stood down from the position of chairman of Llandysul Angling Association. This is therefore also a great opportunity to thank everyone associated with the club for the tremendous support and encouragement I have received. I could wish for nothing better for my successor, Dr Ian Thomas, than that he should benefit from the kind of help and encouragement that I was so fortunate to receive.

Pat O'Reilly

Contents

Acknowledgements

Many people have contributed ideas, information and pictures for this book, and to mention a few without specifically thanking each one is always unsatisfactory. So I must begin with a special thank you to everyone who has offered contributions. Space limitations have prevented me from including all that was submitted, but please rest assured that your help is appreciated: those things that have been excluded have most definitely influenced what *is* included.

The late Artie Jones, secretary of Llandysul A A for nearly 40 years, contributed most of the information about the development of the club; committee minutes secretary and professional photographer Melvin Grey generously contributed pictures of birds of the Teifi Valley from his extensive wildlife photo library; and committee member Dewi Roberts kindly gave permission for reproduction of eighteenth century engravings of Teifi Valley scenes. Many thanks to you all.

To Tonlas Evans, Llandysul A A's hon. Sec. *extraordinaire*, whose proofreading skills applied to newsletters reduce my typos to what I hope are an acceptable minimum, a special thank you for ploughing through the substantial workload that a book like this represents. For what is now correct, much credit is due to Tonlas; for any slips that remain the responsibility is mine and, in advance, I must express my thanks for readers' tolerance.

CHAPTER 1
The Teifi Valley past and present

What a magnificent river! Flowing some seventy-five miles from a source 1500 feet up in the Cambrian Mountains to its estuary at Cardigan, the Teifi, Queen of Rivers, is both wild and wonderful. Tripping over shallow riffles, roaring through white-water gorges, cascading over thundering waterfalls, drifting lazily through dark pools flanked by lush pastures - in its diversity of scenery and wildlife, the Teifi fully deserves the description unique. This book is as much about that uniqueness as it is about the wealth of opportunity that the Teifi provides for high quality game fishing.

The river begins its journey at Llyn Teifi, one of five natural lakes that make up Teifi Pools. The lakes abound with wild brown trout, most weighing less than a pound but there is just the occasional surprise to add sparkle to a day's fishing.

Llyn Teifi, with the dam wall at the far side

Llyn Teifi before the dam was built (18th century etching)

Llyn Teifi itself provides a supply of water to communities in the upper valley; the other main water resources abstraction is at Llechryd, three miles from the tidal estuary of the river.

The abbey ruins at Strata Florida (18th century etching)

A Flyfisher's Guide to the Teifi Valley

The upper Teifi commands a prominent place in the history of Wales. Strata Florida Abbey – some of the arches of this twelfth-century abbey are still standing - is the burial place of no less than a dozen Princes of Ceredigion and Deheubarth (south-west Wales).

Today the ruins of Strata Florida Abbey are a focal point for historians and tourist visitors

The mediaeval bard Dafydd ap Gwilym is also said to have been buried in the grounds of the abbey.

Miraculously, this beautiful arch still stands today

Past Strata Florida and on down through the village of Pontrhydfendigaid (Bridge of the Blessed Ford), the Teifi is a small, fast-flowing stream with great scenic beauty but rather modest fish populations compared with those of forty years ago.

Pontrhydfendigaid - the old stone bridge (18th century etching)

Fortunately, work is now in progress to try to restore to the upper Teifi its once famous wild brown trout. Tregaron Angling Club controls much of the fishing on the upper reaches of the Teifi as well as on Teifi Pools and the nearby Llyn Berwyn For many years Tregaron A C has been stocking the upper river with brown trout, and latterly native Teifi fish have been reared for this purpose.

Much still needs to be done to overcome water quality problems, including farm pollution and acidification of some upland feeder streams. In places it might also be necessary to reinstate marginal habitats damaged by erosion and silt pollution caused by over-grazing. Only then, perhaps, will the river once more sustain abundant and healthy stocks of brown trout comparable with those for which Oliver Kite and other famous fishermen used to travel to West Wales for their spring trout fishing.

With help from Environment Agency Wales, the two other large angling clubs on the Teifi - Llandysul A A and Teifi Trout Association - are also involved in restoring the indigenous trout populations. For some years, Llandysul A A reared Teifi-native trout in their own hatchery, while the other clubs stocked with fish reared at Llynyfan Hatchery in the neighbouring Towy catchment. Nowadays the emphasis has move to habitat improvement work and trying to avoid farm pollution – in particular sheep dip chemicals that kill off insect life and in some instances are also toxic to fish.

Cors Caron and Tregaron

Although the Teifi is a spate river, and hence prone to large fluctuations in flow as rainfall varies, during dry periods the Teifi's level holds up rather better than that of many Welsh rivers. The reason is Cors Goch Glanteifi, the great red bog of Tregaron. This huge raised bog acts as a sponge, storing water during wet weather and gradually releasing it over a period of a few weeks. Land drainage has reduced this buffering effect and made the Teifi more 'flashy' than it used to be, but anglers still have good reason to be grateful for the presence of Tregaron Bog: without it the lower Teifi would be even more prone to flow fluctuations.

Tregaron bog is also of great interest to conservationists: it is a wonderful nature reserve. A walk along the disused railway track provides a chance to see many lovely wildflowers, animals and birds including, of course, the red kite for which this part of Wales has been a vital last stronghold.

The little market town of Tregaron was once a staging post for the drovers, who used to rest and refresh themselves there before continuing their journey across the bleak Abergwesyn Pass.

Between Tregaron and Lanybydder the Teifi winds a gentle path through meadows where cattle graze in summer; sheep, brought down from the hills for lambing, take their place during the winter months. At Llanfair Clydogau, rich ranunculus (water crowfoot) beds give the river a chalkstream aura in summer, and there the insect life is naturally more diverse and abundant than on other reaches. Just below the village, Llandysul A A has its first fishing beat - at Pentre Farm. Four more beats provide members with fishing opportunities before the Teifi reaches the university town of Lampeter. There, from Pont Steffan Bridge downstream for more than four miles on both banks, the club has continuous fishing rights.

Llandewi Brefi (18th century etching)

It was at Lampeter, in the late 1980s, that Llandysul A A carried out a major tree-planting programme to help stabilise the eroding river banks and, at the same time, to increase the habitat diversity of the river. Many of the trees are nearing maturity, and now they are able to fend for themselves without the need for the protective fencing that has saved them from being eaten by cattle and sheep. The fences should remain, however, because they ensure that marginal vegetation can flourish, and without this the river would lose valuable insect habitat. These 'buffer strips', as they are termed, also act as filters and limit the amount of soil and farm chemicals entering the river during heavy rain.

Llandysul A A has several other fisheries along the meandering Teifi between Lampeter and Llanybydder. Here the deep pools and sparkling riffles, interspersed with ranunculus- and starwort-rich glides provide ideal habitat for trout, sea trout and salmon.

For many a year traders have come to the little market town of Llanybydder to buy and sell ponies, steeds and working horses. Today the market, while less busy than fifty years ago, is still an important gathering place for country folk from far and near.

The riverside church at Maesycrugiau

Soon after leaving Llanybydder, the river thunders through the rocky gorge of Maesycrugiau. The old church looks down from its knoll above dense woodland that lines the river above Maesycrugiau Bridge (Pontllwni). Thereafter, the Teifi retains this moody nature: miles of calm meanders and pool-riffle sequences interrupted by narrow gorges at Llandysul, Pentrecwrt, Henllan, Newcastle Emlyn and Cenarth.

Llandysul to Newcastle Emlyn

Llandysul Bridge (18ᵗʰ century etching)

Llandysul itself is on the right (Ceredigion) bank of the Teifi, while its sister village of Pontweli sits on the Carmarthenshire bank below Llandysul Bridge. A fine riverside park and playing field facility, plus a thriving village hall, make Llandysul a natural centre for recreational activities.

The white-water slalom course below Llandysul Bridge

Apart from Llandysul Angling Association there is an active cricket club in the village and a canoe club based on the white-water slalom course at Pont Tyweli.

Llandysul Angling Association owns most of the fishing rights both upstream and downstream of Llandysul village, and this productive section of the river has contributed much to the Teifi's reputation as Wales's premier all-round game fishery. Thirty years ago there was excellent trout fishing on the Teifi between Lampeter and Tregaron. Nowadays most of the resident brown trout have disappeared from the upper reaches, and so it is mainly to Maesycrugiau and Llanfihangel-ar-Arth that club members turn for the best of the trout fishing. Early in the season, March brown and grannom hatches are usually dense in this region, while during the more difficult dog days of summer the great diversity of aquatic and terrestrial insect life provides a challenge to anyone keen on matching the hatch.

Willie Lloyd James with the 8lb brown trout he caught on Llandysul A A waters in July 1954

The varied nature of the river in the Llandysul area means that you can see a wide variety of wildlife without having to travel far. Within a mile of the village, there are pools more than twenty feet deep, white-water narrows, tree-lined glides, and rippling crystal shallows where the Teifi skips through rich green pastures. Otters, kingfishers and dippers add sparkle to a day beside the river - but more of that later.

The gorge at Rhydygalfe – arguably the Teifi's finest sea trout stretch

Along the ten miles of river from Llandysul through Pentrecwrt and Pentrecagal - the latter was the scene of a skirmish during the Rebecca Riots - and on down to Newcastle Emlyn, the club has five more fisheries, each with its own unique personality and distinctive scenery. The old bridge and mill above Alltcafan Gorge, near Pentrecwrt, provide an austere backdrop to one of Llandysul A A's most productive salmon fishing beats.

An 18th century etching of the Newcastle Emlyn's 'new' castle

A Flyfisher's Guide to the Teifi Valley

Newcastle Emlyn is a bustling market town. Bordered on three sides by the River Teifi are the ruins of a fifteenth-century castle, largely demolished by Cromwell's Roundheads in 1644. The original 'New Castle', built in 1240 on the site of an even older fortress, overlooks a picturesque weir upstream of the town.

The weir at Newcastle Emlyn

From Newcastle Emlyn to the tidal limit at Llechryd, the Teifi has high banks and a series of meanders that result in some very deep pools.

Cenarth Falls (18th century etching)

A Flyfisher's Guide to the Teifi Valley

Teifi Trout Association has much of the fishing in this area, including a 'worm-fishing only' stretch just below Cenarth Falls. TTA impose a 'one salmon per day' bag limit on this fishery as a conservation measure.

Cenarth Falls in the summer of 2004

Spectacular falls at Cenarth provide an opportunity for people to watch salmon and sea trout leaping as they make their way up the River Teifi. Most of the fish run at night, and so around dusk is usually a good time to see this migration spectacle.

October 2004, when Cenarth Falls almost became Cenarth Flats

When the Teifi is in full spate, every part of the lovely bridge at Llechryd, four miles downstream from Newdcastle Emlyn, disappears under water and the main A484 road to Cardigan is closed to traffic.

Llechryd Bridge in low water. In a major flood it disappears entirely!

The tidal reaches

Unlike most spate rivers, the Teifi has a very short tidal estuary. Cilgerran Gorge, a mere four miles up from the sea, acts as a bottleneck for spate water, and during heavy rainfall this constriction often results in serious flooding from Llechyd Bridge right up to Cenarth Falls.

Cilgerran Castle is mentioned in history as far back as 1165 and was fought over by Llewelyn the Great and by Owain Glyndwr. The castle has inspired writers and artists through the ages, and it is featured in one of Turner's great paintings.

In the narrow gorge, overlooked by the castle ruins, is evidence of what was once a major industry in this part of Wales. We tend to think of North Wales as the centre of slate mining in Britain, and indeed at its peak of activity well over 80 per cent of the slate mined in Britain came from that area; however, Pembrokeshire also had a significant slate industry as far back as 1566, and there were around 100 slate quarries in operation in Pembrokeshire in the second half of the nineteenth century, and prominent among these were the Cilgerran slate mines.

The last operational slate quarry in Pembrokeshire was Gilfach Quarry, which produced green slate for roofing until as recently as 1987.

Beside the river, near Cilgerran Castle, is a riverside walk with interpretation panels describing the slate quarry industry and the wildlife of the River Teifi in its tidal reaches. The 200-yard path down to the riverside is signposted from the village, or you can start at Llechryd Bridge and take a longer, shady stroll downstream to Cilgerran and on towards the Wildlife Centre just upstream of Cardigan.

The remains of a jetty used by slate barges in Cilgerran Gorge

About 120 years ago there were over 300 coracle fishers on the Teifi; today 12 licensed coracles still work on the tidal river. They fish at night from bowl-shaped boats made with canvass stretched over willow frames and coated with pitch.

Cilgerran Castle and the tidal gorge (18th century etching)

Below Cilgerran, the river drifts through the marshy wildlife reserve before passing the market town of Cardigan. A 15th century five-arched bridge spans the Teifi at Cardigan, overshadowed by the bleak remains of a mediaeval castle. Today a stone otter stands beside Prince Charles Quay, a quiet place where you are quite likely to see more active otters on a summer evening. The quay was once a busy place, with sailing ships docking to unload salted fish and take on cargoes of Cilgerran slate.

Cardigan Bridge is ignored by the otter, whose attention appears to be focussed on passers by on the riverside footpath... and vice versa

From Cardigan it is but a short glide past St Dogmaels to the headland at Gwbert-on-Sea on the north bank of estuary and Poppit Sands on the south, from where the waters of the River Teifi pour out into Cardigan Bay. The estuary is a haven for sea birds and other marine wildlife.

On either side of the mouth of the Teifi the coastland is spectacular. To the south lies Pembrokeshire, with its much-walked Coast Path, while to the north are the equally rugged but much less frequented cliffs of Ceredigion, lacking only a public access path along the cliffs. In places, however, there are sections with footpaths – Mwnt is one example – and for anyone interested in watching seals with their pups this part of the Welsh coastline offers unrivalled opportunity.

Opened in 1970, the Pembrokeshire Coast Path National Trail traverses 186 miles of stunningly beautiful coastal scenery. The Coast Path lies mainly within the Pembrokeshire Coast National Park, and the Park Authority maintains the footpath, which runs from St Dogmaels in the north to Amroth in the south, passing beside the only Marine Nature Reserve in Wales. In spring, the cliff-top wildflowers along the Coast Path are magnificent and well worth a visit, especially with a camera.

Low tide at dusk, Gwbert on Sea

Seals, dolphins and porpoises are a common sight from the rocks at Gwbert and can sometimes be spotted from the beach at Poppit, while bird-watchers can enjoy guided trips to Skomer and Skokolm, island sanctuaries off the Pembrokeshire coast.

The Teifi Estuary, seen from the cliffs at Gwbert-on-Sea

CHAPTER 2
Llandysul A A Fisheries
- a beat-by-beat guide

With some 30 miles of fishing, it's not easy for new members to get to know the various beats, their access and parking. Where are you most likely to catch trout, salmon or sea trout at different times of the year? What is the terrain like? Where are the best pools and runs? And what is the wading like?

This chapter of the book is in the form of a journey along Llandysul A A's waters on the River Teifi, beginning at Llanfair Clydogau near Tregaron and continuing on down through Cellan, Lampeter, Llanybydder, Maesycrugiau, Llandysul, Pentrecwrt, Henllan and Llandyfriog. I hope that it will at least give you a reasonable idea of what to expect when you visit the various fishing beats.

Beat Locations

For each of the beats marked on this location map I have included an illustrated guide and a more detailed beat map. Aerial photographs are also included for several of the beats owned, or in one or two instances leased, by Llandysul A A.

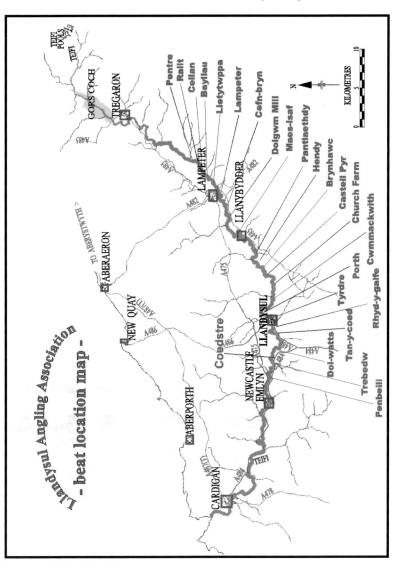

Pentre Farm (Beat 1)

A deep pool near the centre of Pentre Farm beat

Our Pentre Farm beat marks the upper limit of Llandysul AA fishing on the River Teifi. Here the river is less than half the size of the Teifi at Llandysul. The current is swift, and a wide variety of in-stream submerged vegetation, including ranunculus and starwort, makes for ideal trout habitat. In spring this beat has a very good grannom hatch, while the mainstay of the summer trout fishing is provided by moderate hatches of medium olives and spurwings during the day with large sedge flies – Caperer and Large Cinnamons in particular – as darkness descends.

Even this far up river the wading can be difficult and care is needed, especially after a summer spate; there are deep pools on the bends in the watercourse and the current in places is remarkably strong. Most of the riverbed is sandy, but a few large boulders await the unwary, particularly on the deeper side of the river where water rushes in to the necks of pools.

Salmon and sea trout travel through this beat towards the end of the season; however, for most of the year it is as a wild brown trout fishery that we most value our beat at Pentre Farm.

Statistics
Beat 1, the Pentre Farm fishery, comprises a mile and a quarter of fishing on the left bank of the Teifi. This is a rented beat.

Beat limits
The upper limit is half a mile below Llanfair Clydogau Bridge and the lower limit adjoins our Rallt fishery about a mile north of the village of Cellan.

A Flyfisher's Guide to the Teifi Valley

Access and parking
This beat is accessed from the B4343 Cwmann to Llanfair Clydogau road, via a farm gate opposite the lane to Pentre Farm. A Llandysul A A sign marks the access point.

Access is via the left-hand gate

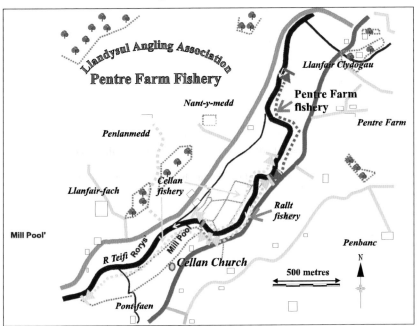

Rallt Farm (Beat 1a)

At Rallt the Teifi is fairly shallow with ranunculus beds along most of the beat. Much of this bank is tree-lined, making thigh waders almost essential.

Trout fishing in wilderness country

Statistics
This rented fishery comprises 500 yards of left-bank fishing and joins together our Pentre and Cellan fisheries.

Trout fishing at Rallt Farm

Fishing the run into a deep pool

Access
Access is from the B4343 Cwmann to Llanfair Clydogau road.

Please close the gate and keep the entrance clear for farm vehicles

A Flyfisher's Guide to the Teifi Valley

Parking

The Association has not been able to secure a private car park at this beat for use by members. It may therefore be necessary, for safety considerations, to park some distance away from the fishery access in order to avoid causing an obstruction on what is in most places a very narrow lane. If you can cope with a walk of nearly half a mile, there is safe, off-road parking at our Pentre Farm fishery (the next beat upstream from the Rallt fishery).

Please ensure when parking that access to farm gates is not restricted: farm vehicles may need to enter the fields beside the river.

Beat limits

Llandysul AA end-of-beat signs mark the limits of this fishery, which is adjoined by our Pentre Farm beat on the upper limit and by our Cellan beat (left bank) on the lower limit.

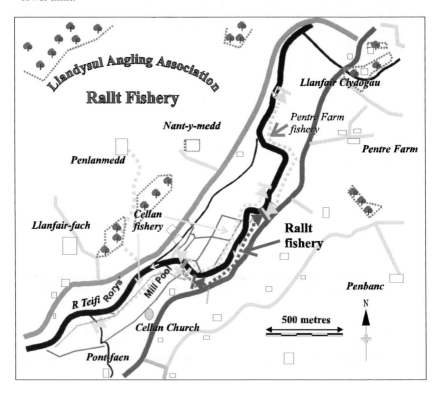

Cellan Fishery (Beat 2)

This is a good brown trout fishery. In many places mature trees shade the river, which races swiftly, making dry fly fishing challenging but all the more rewarding.

A deep glide on the Cellan beat

Here, you are definitely in Kite's Country. That was the name of a TV programme in the 1960s, when Oliver Kite showed viewers how to catch Teifi trout in springtime.

Statistics
The Cellan fishery comprises a mile and a half of fishing, some being on the right-hand bank, some on the left-hand bank, and, over two short stretches, some being double-bank fishing. We purchased the fishing rights to the Cellan fishery in 1978.

Access and parking
This beat is accessed from the B4343 Cwmann to Llanfair Clydogau road a quarter of a mile upstream of Cellan Church. Please obtain permission before parking beside the cottage near to our access point. Parking is also possible on the lane, but you will need to tuck in close to the verge. Please do not block farm gateways.

End-of-beat markers
Llandysul A A end-of-beat signs mark the upper and lower limits of the fishery.

A Flyfisher's Guide to the Teifi Valley

A late spring day on the Cellan fishery

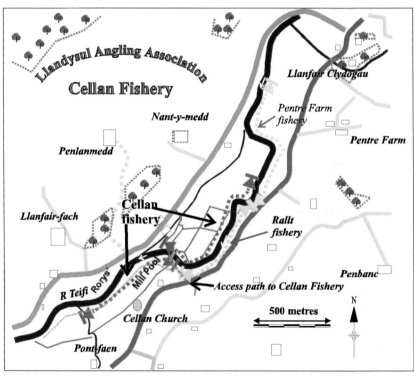

Bayliau Fishing (Beat 2a)

At Bayliau the faster, streamy water is ideal trout habitat. Mature trees overhang the river in places, and on bright days trout sometimes will rise freely there when the rest of the beat is inactive.

Trout fishing near the top of Bayliau fishery

There are several deep pools towards the centre of this beat that hold salmon and sea trout, particularly towards the back end of the season.

Over most of the beat the back cast is clear

Statistics

The Bayliau fishery, comprising some 700 yards of left-bank fishing on the Teifi a mile upstream of Pont Steffan Bridge, Lampeter, is one of our rented fisheries.

Summer trout fishing on a pool at the upper limit of the beat

Ranunculus beds on the lower half of the Bayliau beat provide trout with shade and food on sunny days

A Flyfisher's Guide to the Teifi Valley

Access and Parking

Access is via the B4343
Cwmann to Llanfair
Clydogau road, and
there is room to park on
the wide verge

Beat limits

Llandysul A A end-of-beat signs mark the upper and lower limits of this fishery.

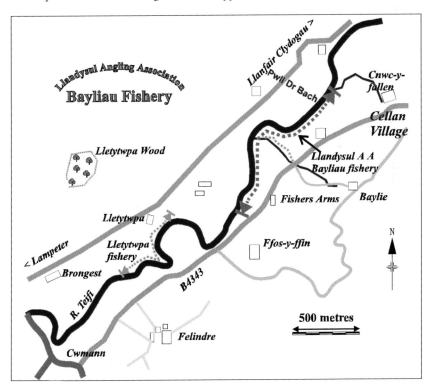

Llettytwpa (Beat 3)

This fishery contains some excellent trout habitat, with water crowfoot beds for which this part of the Teifi has long been famous.

A fast run near the top of the beat

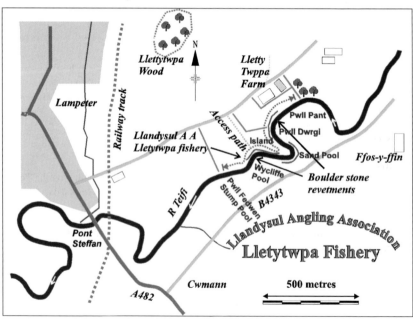

High banks make wading a near necessity

Fishing from the bank is possible over most of the lower half of the beat. At the lower limit, the river is fairly slow flowing and wading is possible, but chest waders are advisable.

There are five salmon pools on this beat. The upper half of the fishery is characterised by sharp bends and deep pools with fast water between them. Revetments (constructed mainly of boulder stone) have had the effect of narrowing the river channel, and so it is both swift and deep. The banks are high, and this makes chest waders essential if you intend wading; however, do note that the current here is very strong and so a wading staff is also strongly recommended.

Statistics
The Lletytwpa fishery, comprising some 700 yards of right-bank fishing on the Teifi a mile upstream of Pont Steffan Bridge, Lampeter, is one of our rented beats.

Access and parking
This beat is accessed via a gate some 100 yards west (downstream) of the farm of Lletty Twppa (one of many spellings of the name!), on the Lampeter to Llanfair Clydogau road, a mile outside Lampeter.

Please tuck your car close in to the verge when parking on the lane, and avoid parking on bends or close to farm gateways where farm vehicles may need to enter or leave the fields while you are fishing.

Please leave the farm gate clear when parking

Beat Limits

Llandysul A A end-of-beat signs mark the upper and lower limits of the fishery.

The upper limit of the Llettytwpa beat

Lampeter Waters (Beat 4)

This is one of our most scenic stretches, with ranunculus beds and a range of bank-side trees and plants. It is mainly double-bank fishing.

Trout fishing at Pwll Felinfach

The beat includes several famous and productive salmon and sea trout pools including Pwll Bili, Pwll Beili-goch and Pwll Felinfach. There are also several ranunculus-rich glides where the trout fishing can be good even on bright days.

To arrest erosion we have planted trees and put up protective fencing in places, and these now provide rich marginal habitat for birds and many other kinds of wildlife. Nevertheless, there are still stretches where erosion makes the banks unsafe, especially after heavy rain in spring and autumn, and so it is advisable to keep well away from the edge at such times.

In the Lampeter area the River Teifi is particularly prone to bursting its banks during periods of wet weather, particularly in autumn. For this reason, in high-water conditions that might still be fishable on beats further downstream the Lampeter Waters fishing can become inaccessible. Fortunately the river level falls back quite quickly in this area, and it usually fines down and gets into good fishing condition a day or so before the river around Llandysul is clear enough for fishing.

Statistics
Beat 4, comprising some four miles of double-bank fishing on the Teifi at Lampeter, became part of the Llandysul A A waters when Lampeter Angling Association joined with our club in April 1970.

A fine summer sewin

The Lampeter beat tends to be good for brown trout early in the season and better for sewin from late July onwards.

Summer on the Teifi at Lampeter

Trout fishing at the upper beat limit

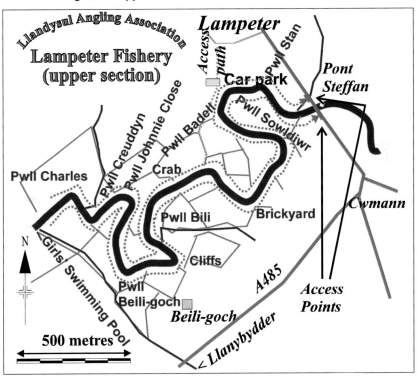

Access and parking

The top part of the beat can be reached via a farm gate on the left-hand bank at Lampeter Bridge (Pont Steffan). Please do not park on the road near the bridge; it is a humpbacked bridge and already quite hazardous.

On the right-hand bank there is an access path to the top of the beat from Cae Dash, where in 2003 the Association built its own private car park for use by club members and permit holders.

The lower part of the fishery is accessible from the left-hand bank at Felinfach, where the club has a car park. Members are requested not to use the private drive, and to close farm gates when crossing the fields.

Be prepared for a walk of some 400 yards to the river. The fields are generally well tended but there are several humps and dips that could be a problem for anyone unsteady on their feet. The Felinfach access point also serves our Cefn-bryn fishery, which adjoins the Lampeter fishery on its left bank.

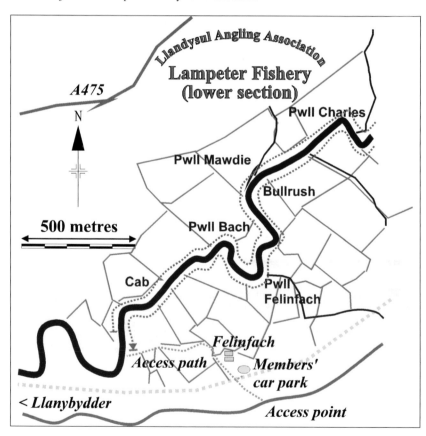

Cefn-bryn Waters (Beat 5)

Near the top of this beat, weedy runs provide good trout habitat. The banks are clear, making for easy casting. Deep pools in the middle of the beat are interspersed with swift glides where summer sewin can sometimes be taken in daytime.

Fast, streamy water below Hollybush Pool

Late summer fishing as dusk descends

A Flyfisher's Guide to the Teifi Valley

Statistics
Cefn-bryn fishery, beat 5, comprising 880 yards of left-bank fishing on the Teifi downstream of Lampeter, was purchased in October 1976.

Access and parking
The fishing is accessed via our private car park beside the A485 Cwmann to Llanybydder road, near the farmhouse of Cefn-bryn.

Beat limits
An end-of-beat sign marks the point where the Cefn-bryn fishing adjoins Llandysul A A's Lampeter fishery on the left bank of the river near to Llwyn-on.

The lower beat limit, some 200 yards downstream of a point where the river runs close to the old railway track, is also marked with a Llandysul A A sign. There the river is deep and slow, and wading is not recommended.

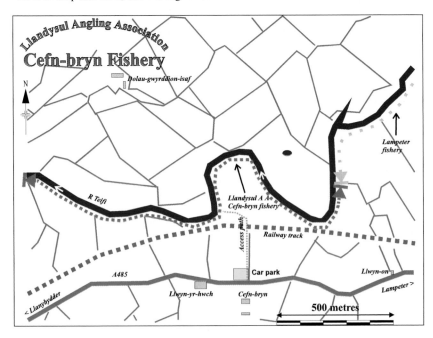

- 42 -

Dolgwm Mill Waters (Beat 6)

At Dolgwm Mill, half a mile east of Llyn Pencarreg on the A485, Llandysul A A's Beat 6 comprises one right bank meadow and five left bank meadows.

A deep pool near the top of the beat

There are deep pools near the upper and lower limits of this beat and a good variety of other fishing opportunities. In spring there are dense hatches of grannom sedge, and sometimes enough March Browns to cause a good daytime rise in early April. Dry fly fishing for trout can be very productive at such times.

Later in the year - generally after the end of June - the sewin arrive. On some of the tree-lined stretches it is possible to tempt them quite early in the evening; elsewhere, flyfishing at night is usually the best approach. The well-shaded pools near the lower beat limit are always a good place to try for a sewin. In autumn, the swift glides in the middle of the beat often hold shoals of whitling, which will rise readily to dry flies in dull weather or when rain has added a hint of colour to the water.

Statistics
Dolgwm Mill fishery, three miles north west of Llanybydder on the A485, extends more than a mile and includes more then 300 yards of double-bank fishing. We purchased this beat in December 1977.

Salmon fishing near the top of the beat

Clear banks over most of the beat make it an ideal venue for anyone
who is new to flyfishing

Access and parking

The access is off the A485 Llanybydder to Lampeter road some 300 yards west of Dolgwm. There is an orange Llandysul A A beat sign on a tree at the left-hand side of the entrance to our private car park, which has space for up to six cars.

The access path runs beside a sheep-dipping station and through a pair of farm gates. To get to the top of the beat, turn right via the next farm gate and cross one meadow until you reach the river. For the lower section of the beat, walk past the sheep-dipping facility and on along the hedgerow until you reach the river.

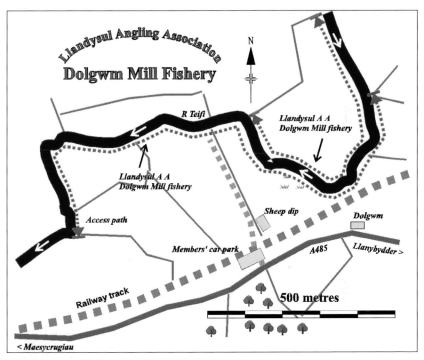

Beat limits are marked by Llandysul A A signs. (The picture on the left shows the lower limit on the left-hand bank.)

Maesisaf Waters (Beat 7)

Maesisaf fishery comprises seven meadows (approximately one mile) of left-bank fishing. There are plenty of good streamy runs on this fishery and some splendid salmon pools near the top of the beat. The fishing extends along seven meadows.

Napier Pool, a noted salmon hotspot at the lower end of Maes-isaf

Salmon holding water near the top of the beat

Summer on the middle of the beat

Statistics

We purchased this fishery in January 1992. The fishing extends to more than a mile of single-bank fishing on the left bank of the river. Most of the fishing is on a sweeping bend where the water is shallower on our bank and deeper on the far side.

Access and parking

Access is via a lane near the Pencarreg 40 mph sign on the A485 Llanybydder to Cwmann road.

Club members have a private car park near to the disused railway track. Go through the gate at the rear of our car park, cross the field to a small stream, and follow that stream into the next field. A double fence marks the lower limit.

The Association's private car park at the Maesisaf fishery

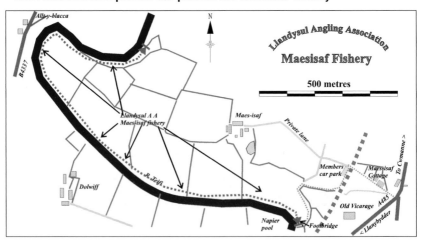

Beat limits
Orange end-of-beat signs mark the upper and lower limits of the fishery.

Hendy fishery (Beat 7-1)

This beat offers plenty of good salmon, sea trout and trout fishing. Over most of the beat the riverbank is clear of trees, making it practicable to fish from the banks.

Pwll Craig y Lantarn in summer

Trout fishing near the top of the beat

Pwll Craig-y-Lantarn is a noted salmon and sea trout hotspot. There is also some excellent salmon fishing at the topmost meadow of this beat, and the pool at the top of the beat is a noted sewin hotspot.

For trout fishers, the fast runs beside the islands are particularly good, although the casting is inevitably tricky. There are several large beds of ranunculus near the top of the beat and they are home to some nice wild brown trout.

Statistics

The Hendy fishery is held on a leasing agreement. The beat comprises a mile and a quarter of single-bank fishing. The fishing extends along a short stretch of dense woodland and a further five meadows.

Access and parking

There is limited opportunity for parking within the village of Rhuddlan; however, there are places on the lanes just outside the village where members can park without obstructing the road.

Access is beside Lantern Lodge, and signs are visible from the road. Members should pass quietly beside the Lodge after night fishing and close the gate to our access path. The path takes you beside a 'Tolkienesque' wood and a towering rock cliff that always makes it very dark there even on moonlit nights; a good torch is therefore needed if you intend fishing this beat at night.

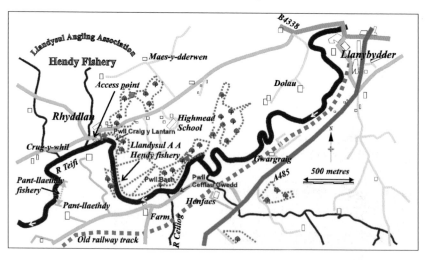

Beat limits

The lower limit is marked by a Llandysul A A end-of-beat sign near the start of the access footpath that runs beside Lantern Lodge. The upper limit is marked by an end-of-beat sign mounted on a tree at the boundary of a wood.

Pantllaethdy (Beat 7a)

This productive but very underused fishery has swift glides providing the turbulence that makes it possible to catch salmon and sea trout even on bright days.

Deep water near the outside of a sharp bend

The lower beat limit

Statistics

Pantllaethdy fishery, two miles from Maesycrugiau, is mid-way between our Brynhawc and Hendy beats; we bought it in May 1992. There are three main pools: one at each end of the beat and a third, somewhat shallower pool near the mid point. In places casting from the bank is necessary, as the deep, fast-flowing water makes wading hazardous on this ideal daytime fishery.

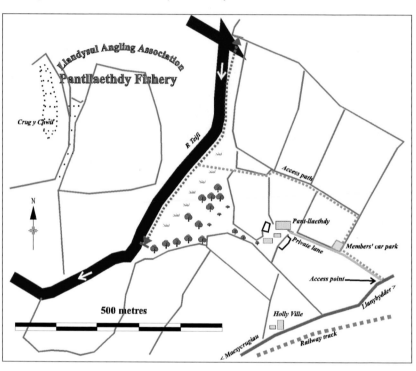

Access and parking

Our car park is 150 yards down a lane from the Llanybydder to Maesycrugiau road. To reach the river, follow the path from the back of the car park around one field and across three more small fields.

Brynhawc Waters (Beat 8)

This is a productive fishery from the start of the season, as salmon and large sea trout tend to rest in Jack's Pool. This fishery includes several other famous salmon and sea trout pools, and there are also some excellent brown trout stretches.

There is plenty of easy bank fishing throughout most of this beat

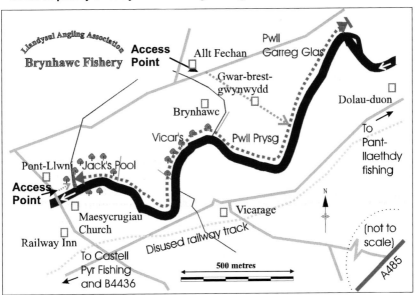

Safety rails and steps at Jack's Pool

Rich ranunculus beds in shallower stretches provide an abundance of insect life.

The view looking downstream over Jack's Pool

Access and parking
Access to the bottom half of this beat is via a stile and footpath on the right-hand bank upstream from Maesycrugiau Bridge. There is a limited amount of parking space at the end of the bridge; please park to avoid obstructing the road.

Dusk descending over Pwll Prysg

Half way up the beat, the path through the wood can be difficult, especially in wet weather. Better access to the upper stretch is via Gwarbrest-Gwynwydd Farm, at Allt Fechan, but note that the meadow slopes quite steeply down to the river.

Statistics

Brynhawc, comprising 1.5 miles of fishing on the right bank of the Teifi at Maesycrugiau, was purchased in April 1975.

Rules

Jack's Pool, the first deep pool upstream of Pontllwni (the road bridge at Maesycrugiau), is subject to the 'Odds-and-Evens' restriction. Members and visitors with odd numbered tickets may fish there from noon on odd numbered days of the month until noon the following day. (Vice-versa for holders of even-numbered permits.) The fishing from Pwll Prysg down through Vicar's to the run above Jack's Pool is designated 'fly only'.

Beat limits

Our fishing starts after the first 100 yards of fast water above Pontllwni (Maesycrugiau Bridge); orange Llandysul A A end-of-beat signs on trees denote the upper and lower beat limits of the fishery.

Castell Pyr (Beat 8a)

The Castell Pyr beat is unsuitable for infirm anglers. A steep-sided wood abuts the lower part of the fishing, and much of the riverbed is rocky with difficult wading.

A glide at the top of the beat usually holds small sewin in summer

The pool at the bottom of Castell Pyr fishery

The pool at the lower limit of the beat is deep; salmon rest in the quiet back eddies in summer and on the pool tail in autumn. Spey casting is necessary there.

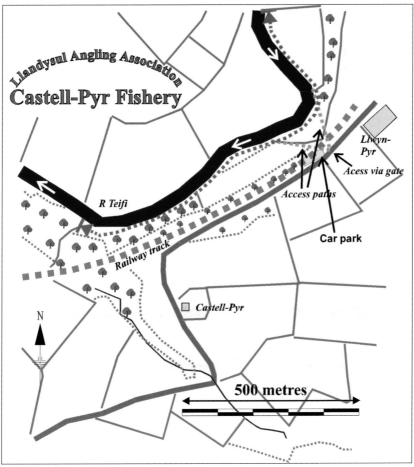

Llandysul Angling Association
Castell-Pyr Fishery

Llwyn-Pyr

Acess via gate

Access paths

R Teifi

Car park

Railway track

N

Castell-Pyr

500 metres

A fast-flowing run near the top of the beat

Statistics

In August 1994 we purchased this 650-yard, left-bank beat together with a nearby cottage; the cottage was subsequently sold.

Access and parking

The club's private car park and the access gate to the fishery, near Llwyn Pyr Farm

Beat limits

The upper and lower limits of the fishery are marked by orange end-of-beat signs.

Church Farm Fishery (Beat 9)

The Church Farm fishery comprises four meadows at Llanfihangel-ar-Arth. It is a particularly productive salmon fishery but can also be good for sea trout.

Vicar's Pool, near the top of the beat, is noted for its autumn salmon

A fast glide in the middle of Church fishery

A Flyfisher's Guide to the Teifi Valley

Statistics

In July 1988 we purchased this beat, comprising half a mile of left-bank fishing.

Access and parking

Access is via Wernmackwith Farm and Cwmmackwith fishery, where we have a private car park for Llandysul A A members and visitors. (There is no access from Llanfihangel Bridge.) 100 yards up the hill from our car park, cross a stile, go through the woods, and continue on upstream across a footbridge and past Ladies Pool, Oak Pool and Clettwr Run. You are then on the Church Farm fishery.

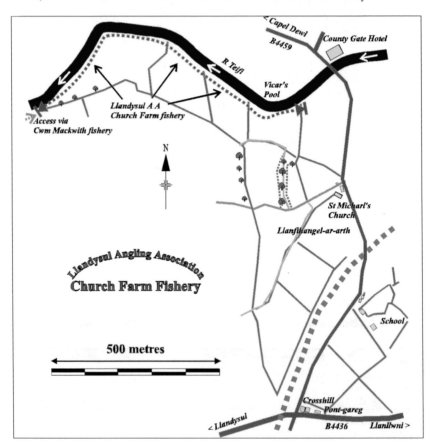

Beat limits

The top of Clettwr Run marks the end of the Cwmmackwith Waters and the start of our Church Farm Fishery. Orange marker signs denote the limits of the beat.

Cwmmackwith Fishery (Beat 10)

Famous for its large sea trout and autumn salmon, this is also one of the most scenic stretches of the Teifi. There are also a few good trout spots on this fishery.

Looking downstream towards Escot Pool

Summer success on a streamy section just upstream of Escot Pool

The pool and riffle nature of this beat makes it an ideal autumn salmon fishery. In most places there is no need to wade. In summer, flyfishing at night is the favoured method for sewin, and the tree-lined pools are particularly productive in low-water conditions. The pool where the River Clettwr enters the Teifi has high banks on its left-hand side; this provides good sea trout fishing even on moonlit nights for those able to spey cast.

Evening grilse fishing, Cwmmackwith

Trout in Clettwr Run can give great sport when summer sedges are hatching in the early evening; the ranunculus beds at the top of Ladies Pool are also worth trying, although avoiding 'drag' can be quite a challenge.

Statistics
In 1966 we purchased this beat, which comprises a mile and a half of fishing on the left bank of the Teifi near Llandysul.

Access and parking

Access is via a narrow lane running north off the B4436 Llandysul to Llanfihangel-ar-Arth road

Our private car park close to the Cwmmackwith fishery

Below the farmyard at Wernmackwith, you will pass on your right two small quarries near the bottom of the hill. Please do not park there: they belong to the farmer, who uses them for turning farm vehicles. Our private car park is a further 100 yards down the lane.

Once at our car park, to reach the fishery walk back up the hill for 100 yards. A stile leads to a short path through the woods. Turn right (upstream) and cross a footbridge to get to Ladies Pool, Oak Pool and Clettwr Run; alternatively, turning left (downstream) will bring you down to Escot, Sunday and Plantation Pools.

Ladies Pool at dusk

Beat limits

The run in to Wood Pool, below Plantation, is the lower limit of the Cwmmackwith fishery and marks the start of our Porth Waters fishing, which many locals still refer to as the Dolgrogws Fishery. (NB: there is another Wood Pool immediately downstream of Ladies Pool in the middle of the Cwmmackwith beat. This is rather confusing, but the pool names are historic and many of them have origins now lost in the mists of time.)

The upper limit of the Cwmmackwith fishing is the top of Clettwr Run, where the Cwmmackwith beat adjoins our Church Farm fishery. The upper and lower limits of this fishery are marked by orange Llandysul AA end-of-beat signs fixed to riverside trees.

Rules

The 'odd-and-even' rule applies throughout the Cwmmackwith fishery. Members and visitors having odd-numbered permits are entitled to fish on this beat from 12 noon on odd dates until mid-day the following day. (Vice versa applies to members who hold even-numbered tickets.)

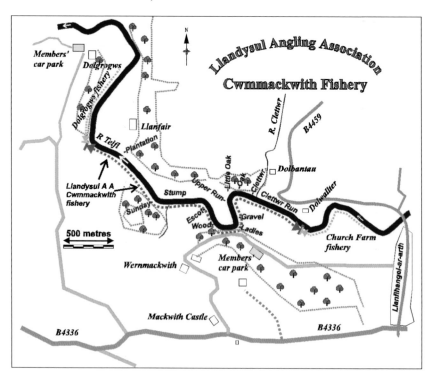

Porth Waters, Dolgrogws (Beat 11)

Porth Waters (the Dolgrogws fishery) provides two miles of fishing from the club's suspension bridge at Abercerdin Flats up to the start of our Cwmmackwith fishery.

Salmon fishing at Wyckhams early in the season

Horse Pool, near Dolgrogws Farm

Sea trout fishing, Wall Pool

Abercerdin Flats, at the lower limit of the beat, can be good for trout in springtime, as can the streamy sections below Horse Pool. The rest of the beat is mainly a salmon and sea trout fishery comprising a sequence of pools and riffles. Near the top of the beat there is a long, slow-flowing stretch known as Wire Flats; it appears largely featureless but is well shaded by trees on the far bank and provides sufficient cover to attract and retain large numbers of sea trout – including some very big ones – throughout the summer months.

At Church Pool, about half a mile upstream of the Dolgrogws Farm access, steeply shelving gravel that presents a potential hazard for the unwary wading angler. At the neck of this pool there is a short stretch of fast water over rounded boulders, and wading there can be particularly hazardous.

Statistics

In October 1973 we bought the Dolgrogws fishing (formerly Porth Waters), comprising nearly two miles of fishing on the left bank of the Teifi near Llandysul. Then in May 1987 we were able to secure the Farmyard fishing at Frongoch to link the Dolgrogws fishery to our Cwmmackwith beat.

Access and parking

There is access to this fishery 500 yards north of Llandysul on the B4476, with a roadside car park for club members. On the eastern side of the road a gate leads across the meadow to our suspension bridge. Our fishing starts immediately upstream of the bridge. The other access point is via the lane to Dolgrogws Farm.

A Flyfisher's Guide to the Teifi Valley

The entrance to the Dolgrogws access road

In partnership with the owners of Dolgrogws Farm we resurfaced the access road that leads down to the fishery. The club's private car park at the bottom of the lane has been left in its natural state, at the request of the owners of the farm; members are asked to park so that access to the field gates is not obstructed.

Our private car park at Dolgrogws

To reach the fishing, enter the farm gate beside the car park. On the far side of a small paddock cross a stile; steep paths go down to the river. The path to the left takes you downstream past Horse Pool; the path to the right takes you upstream past Wall Pool and Padget's to Church Pool and then on to Wire Flats and Wood Pool.

Beat limits
The suspension bridge marks the lower limit of the beat; the upper limit is the top of Wood Pool, below Plantation on the Cwmmackwith beat. Orange marker signs denote the locations of these beat limits.

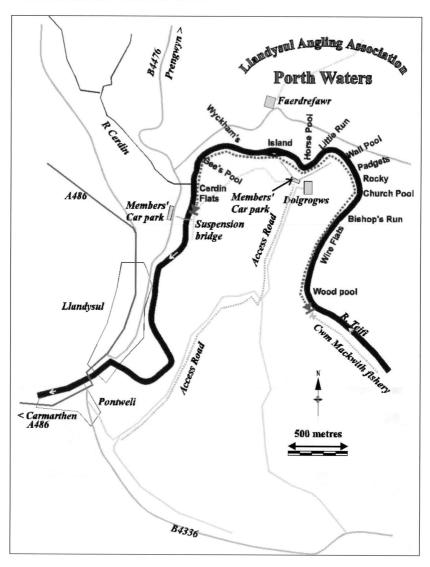

Tyrdref Waters, Llandysul (Beat 12)

By day the top half of this beat is an ideal place for youngsters to learn to fish. In the evenings, however, Tyrdref becomes a very productive summer sea trout fishery.

Young flyfishers at Tyrdref receiving tuition from Eric Davies

The Young Conservationists 'bug hunt' is also held at Tyr Dref fishery

In summer we use this stretch during our free flyfishing lessons for schoolchildren, and in recent years it has also been the venue for our Young Conservationists survey work, involving the study and recording of river ecology and wildlife. Each spring, as part of Llandysul A A's programme of events during its Welcome Days, potential and actual new members of the Association have an opportunity to see casting demonstrations here and to receive introductory river casting tuition.

Welcome Day: casting demonstrations at the Tyrdref fishery

There are two good salmon pools as well as some faster, streamy water that often holds grilse in the summer months. The occasional brown trout above the pound mark is caught on this stretch, too. The river is relatively narrow here and can be fished by fly without the need for wading. Because the banks are high, you may need to get down to the water's edge and to either use roll or Spey casting methods. Spinning is easy here, but beware of low branches on some of the overhanging trees.

In high water, care is necessary at the lower end of the beat, where a swift glide leads to the white-water canoeing slalom course at Pontweli. To fall in at this point could be very dangerous indeed.

Statistics

Beat number 12, the Tyrdref Fishery, comprising 540 yards of single bank fishing on the right (Ceredigionshire) bank of the Teifi at Llandysul, was purchased by the club in January 1981. In conjunction with this purchase, the land comprising the present playing field was also secured for the enjoyment of the people of Llandysul and the many visitors to the village. Cricket, tennis and many other sporting activities take place on well-tended courts and pitches bedside the River Teifi.

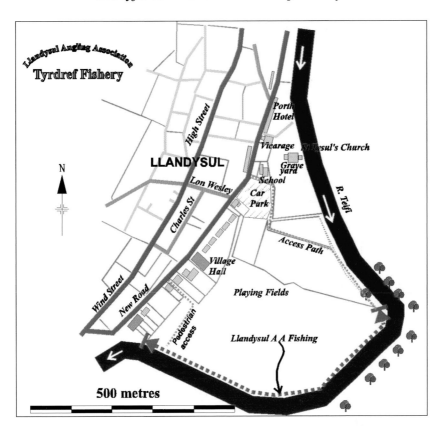

Access and parking

There is vehicle access to parking 50 yards from the riverbank. A ramp leads down to a shingle bank beside a deep pool, providing opportunities for disabled anglers who can obtain Llandysul A A permits for this fishery at a concessionary rate.

The lower part of the Tyrdref fishery at Llandysul

Rhydygalfe Fishery (Beat 13)

On this most productive salmon and sea trout fishery great care is needed on the right-hand bank, to which access is via a rocky gorge.

The tail of the pool below Rhydygalfe Farm

A deep pool in the rocky gorge

The deep, dark gorge holds very big sea trout

Below the canoe slalom rapids, the gorge itself is rocky and stable, and even in low flows the river is in excess of 20 feet deep in some of the narrower pools. Elsewhere steep ledges make wading hazardous.

The gravel bed of the pool below the gorge alters each time there is a big spate, as gravel is carried downstream and deposited there or swept into banks on one side of the river or the other. The fishing here varies significantly from year to year.

Statistics

This beat comprises approximately a mile of fishing on the right-hand bank of the Teifi just below Llandysul Bridge plus a further mile on the left bank. We bought this fishery in September 1994.

Access and parking

On the left bank, there is parking in the lay-by twenty yards downstream of the old railway bridge at Rhydygalfe Farm.

Currently, access to our left-bank fishing at Rhydygalfe is obtained by crossing a field adjacent to the lay-by and then turning left onto the old railway track. (The rails and sleepers have long since been removed.) After proceeding fifteen yards along the track, climb over a stile on the right and cross one meadow to reach the river. The access is likely to change when the Llandysul Bypass is constructed.

The path upstream of Rhydygalfe Farm is through steep woodland and is not recommended for those who are unsure on their feet.

On the right-hand bank, access is from the Ceredigionshire (northern) end of Llandysul Bridge, via a cart track running alongside the river. Parking is possible beside the track.

On the right-hand bank, the route down the gorge is not recommended for anyone who finds rough ground a problem. We have improved the path through a very rocky section of the gorge, but great care is still needed there especially at night. A locked metal gate has been installed to deter unauthorised entry to what is a potentially very dangerous part of the river.

A coded lock secures the access gate to this fishery. Members and visitors are provided with a numerical code (printed upon their permits) which must be entered in order to open the gate.

A Flyfisher's Guide to the Teifi Valley

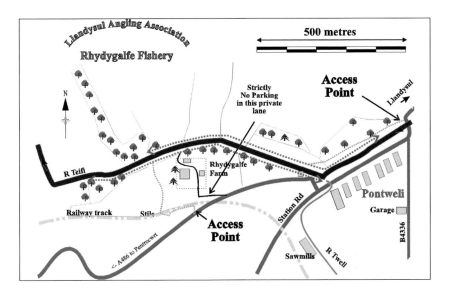

Beat limits

On the left-hand bank, the upper limit is the confluence of the River Tweli. The lower limit is in a fast-water run 200 yards downstream of Rhydygalfe Farmhouse; a fence bearing an end-of-beat marker denotes the boundary. On the right-hand bank, the upper limit is marked by an end-of-beat sign on an oak tree 50 yards below Llandysul Bridge. On the left-hand bank, signs denote the limits of our fishing.

Rules

Members and visitors with odd numbered tickets may fish here only on odd numbered days of the month, starting at noon and stopping before noon on the following day. (Vice versa applies for holders of even permits.)

Rhydygalfe Farm and the lower part of our fishery

Tan-y-Coed Fishery (Beat 13a)

This beat offers something for everyone. The stretch opposite our car park provides good trout fishing and, because the banks are clear and low, it is ideal for beginners learning to cast. The lower 300 yards of the beat hold sea trout all through the season, as do the pools towards the top of the fishery. Pwll Henry, 200 yards from the upper beat limit, is a noted sea trout hotspot.

Good trout habitat near the car park

Pwll Henry

The view looking upstream to Pwll Du

Ray and Cherrie Neale with a summer salmon from Pwll Du

A Flyfisher's Guide to the Teifi Valley

Few salmon pools on the Teifi can challenge Pwll Du, near Tan-y-Coed Farmhouse. The path beside the pool can be hazardous, and care is necessary in the dark or in periods of wet weather. (Stiles at either end of the wood at Pwll Du denote the start and finish of the 'Even-and-Odd' permits rule that applies to this short stretch.)

Statistics

The Tan-y-Coed fishery, comprising two miles of single-bank fishing on the left (Carmarthenshire) bank of the Teifi between Pentrecwrt and Llandysul, was purchased in May 1995.

Access and parking

There is a single access point to this beat from our private car park beside the A486 Pentrecwrt to Llandysul road. Opposite the gate to the car park is a stile bearing a Llandysul AA orange sign.

Llandysul A A's private car park at Tan-y-Coed

The access gate and stile

After crossing the stile, go directly across the field to the riverbank. From there, please keep close to the bank and do not cut across fields in order to avoid walking round meanders in the river course. We agreed this restricted access in return for the private car park that allows members to park their vehicles off the busy main road.

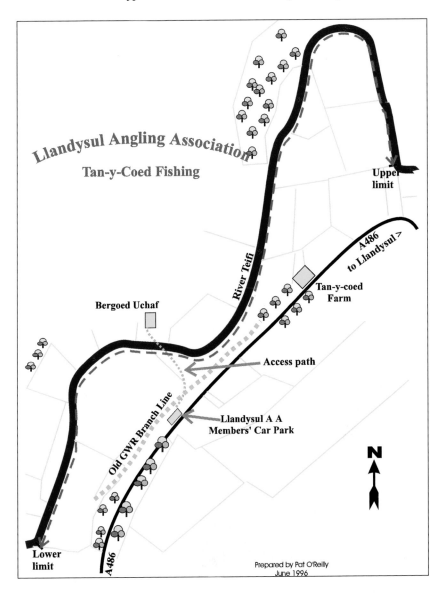

Llandysul Angling Association
Tan-y-Coed Fishing

Upper limit

River Teifi

A486 to Llandysul >

Tan-y-coed Farm

Bergoed Uchaf

Access path

Old GWR Branch Line

Llandysul A A Members' Car Park

N

Lower limit

A486

Prepared by Pat O'Reilly
June 1996

Rules

The fishing between the two stiles at either end of the woods at Pwll Du is subject to the 'Odd and Even' permits rule. Members and visitors with odd-numbered permits may fish there only from 12 noon on odd numbered days of the month until 12 noon the following day (and vice versa for holders of even-numbered permits).

The Dol Watts Fishery (Beat 14)

There is a spectacular view of this fishery from Alltcafan Bridge looking upstream. The village of Pentrecwrt can be seen in the background.

Dol Watts fishery seen from Alltcafan Bridge

The whole beat is visible in this aerial photo

This is an ideal fishery for anyone who enjoys flyfishing but really needs a clear back cast. Over most of this beat the bank is low and devoid of trees. The run in to the pool just above the road bridge can be very productive for sea trout at dusk.

Statistics
This beat, comprising half a mile of right-hand bank fishing at Dol Watts, near Pentrecwrt, was purchased in April 1988.

Access and parking
There is parking near Alltcafan Bridge, and it is possible to reach the lower end of this fishery via a steep bank and stile on the right bank at the upstream side of the bridge. A much easier and only slightly longer route is via the lane running parallel to the river on the right-hand bank (using the same access point as above) and then down the farm track, under the old railway bridge and through a gate. This takes you to the river near the upper limit of our fishing

Beat limits
Our fishing is from the road bridge to a marker on a tree beyond the old railway bridge. At the lower access there is a stile; please do not cross fences at any other locations as this can damage fences and lead to livestock straying and damaging crops. The lower limit of the fishery is denoted by an orange end-of-beat sign beside Alltcafan Bridge and the upper limit by a similar sign on a tree a short distance upstream of the remains of the old railway bridge.

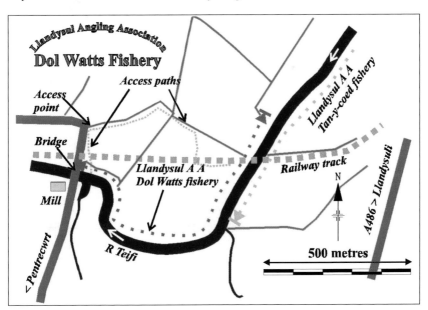

Coedstre Fishery (Beat 14-1)

This very varied left-bank fishery provides good trout fishing in spring and early summer, and it is one of our best early-season sea trout fisheries.

Trout fishing on a streamy run near the bottom of the beat

A very good sea trout pool near the top of the beat

The lower third of the beat is shallow and fast. Above this there is a glide beneath a high bank, where some nice brown trout can be caught on dry fly or nymph. The next pool is deep, slow flowing and well shaded on the far side, making it a first-class sea trout pool, with salmon fishing worth a try at the neck and the tail. We also have the tail of the next pool up, which holds the occasional sewin in summer.

Summer fishing on the middle section of the beat

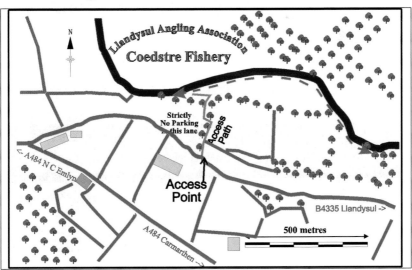

Statistics

This is our most recently acquired fishing beat; it was secured on a leased basis from the start of the 2003 season.

Access and Parking

Space for parking at Coedstre is limited

Access to the Coedstre fishery is via a farm track. There is room for no more than one car on the widened verge near the entry track, and it may be best to park well away from the access and walk to the fishery.

Beat Limits

The upper and lower beat limits are marked by Llandysul A A end-of-beat signs.

Lower beat limit   **Upper beat limit**

Trebedw Fishery (Beat 14a)

This short beat is very productive for sea trout and autumn salmon.

A good sea trout lie near the lower limit of the beat

Casting into a deep gully near the top of the beat

Along the topmost 50 metres of this beat the river is shallow and tree-lined, deepening gradually on our (right) bank. Over the remainder of the beat sea trout tend to lie in a deep gully against the far bank.

Salmon fishing at Trebedw

Although this is not noted as a trout fishery, a few nice fish can be seen rising to sedges on summer evenings. One or two grilse are also caught here each season. The banks are not high, and if you can cast reasonably accurately at distances up to 18 yards, you should be able to cover most of the fishery from the bank.

Statistics
We have been renting this 600-yard fishery, near the village of Henllan, since 1995.

Access and parking
There is a single access path to the fishery, approximately a mile (1.5km) from Henllan Bridge on the B4334. Access is via a lane at Trebedw village, and the access point is marked by an orange Llandysul A A sign. A path with a series of steps leads down to a field gate to the right of Ddol, a private house. There are stiles near each end of our beat, which is fenced off to preclude access by cattle.

Unfortunately there is no Llandysul A A car park on this beat, and club members using the pull-in near the access path are requested to ensure that farm vehicle entry to the field gate is not obstructed.

A Flyfisher's Guide to the Teifi Valley

There is a small area suitable for parking near to the access path

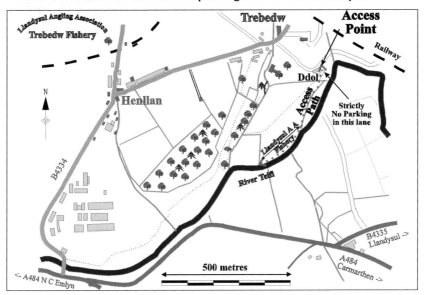

Beat limits

Signs, affixed to riverside trees, mark the upper and lower limits of the beat.

Penbeili fishery (Beat 15)

Over part of this beat we have double-bank fishing. The right bank fishery is a mile or so upstream of Llandyfriog, while on the left bank we have a stretch of fishing at Pentrecagal, some three miles upstream of Newcastle Emlyn.

Searching for a sewin in deep water at Pwll Artie

In summer the lower 300 yards of the right-bank fishing are shallow and ideal for practising casting; in spring this stretch sometimes holds salmon. The rest of the right bank fishery is a sequence of pools and riffles, and provides opportunities for trout, sewin and salmon fishing.

Pwll Artie, mid way along this beat, has high banks and is best fished by wading beneath the trees. A noted sea-trout pool, it has also produced some fine trout including, in 1994, one of over 5 lbs.

At the top of the beat there is a large pool with deep lies on our bank and just one or two places where rocky ledges afford good casting positions. Spinning is very productive here when the river is high. On the left bank, the best of the fishing is in the field below Afon Teifi Caravan Park.

Statistics
This beat, comprising 1320 yards of right bank fishing and 720 yards of left-bank fishing, was purchased in September 1973.

Access and parking

On the right-hand bank, there is parking in a lay-by on the A475 Newcastle Emlyn to Lampeter road a mile east of Llandyfriog. A gate bearing a Llandysul A A sign takes you beneath a railway bridge, through a second gate and down to the river. Our left bank fishing comprises three meadows, including the grounds of Afon Teifi Caravan Park. Access to the left-bank fishing (no vehicles) is via the Caravan Park.

Access to the right-bank fishing   **Parking for our right-bank fishing**

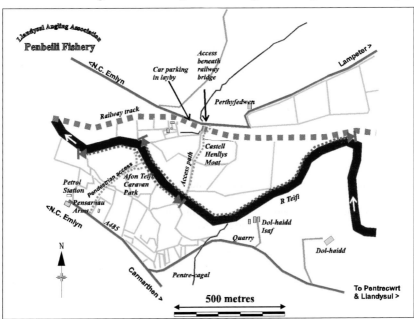

Beat limits

End-of-beat marker signs denote the upper and lower limits of the fishery.

CHAPTER 3
Other Fisheries in the Teifi Valley

Although the main purpose of this book is to help people to enjoy the fishing opportunities provided by Llandysul Angling Association, many of the club's members and visitors also enjoy stillwater trout fishing. Some may even wish to visit other river fisheries on the Teifi, of which the list provided here cannot be exhaustive. There are also several good coarse fishing lakes in or close to the Teifi Valley, and brief details of some of the best of these are also provided. It's not practicable to include comprehensive details and maps of each of these fisheries, but I hope that the address and contact details will prove helpful. Finally, recognising that many people like to fish for bass or other sea species from time to time, I am including a mention of some of the beach and rock shore hotspots and a selection of the charter boats currently operating from ports within a reasonable travelling distance of the Teifi Valley.

Cardigan Island - a great place for sea angling *and* for birdwatching

As a matter of fact...

While there can be no excuse for any serious errors or omissions in the chapters dealing with Llandysul Angling Association and its fishing beats, I am to a very large extent at the mercy of other information sources for contact details and descriptions of some of the other fisheries mentioned in this chapter. If you intend making a trip to visit any of the venues listed here, please telephone beforehand to check. Private fisheries and charter boats do change hands from time to time, so that even information that was correct at the time of going to press could be out of date when you read this book.

At Llys-y-fran Reservoir you can fish for trout from boat or shore

Most of the lowland trout fisheries contain rainbows, but some also have a stock of wild brown trout of the quality shown here.

Stillwater Trout Fisheries

Alltrodyn Trout Lake

A 2-acre catch-and-release trout lake; wheelchair friendly platforms and lodge.
Address: Alltrodyn Trout Lake, Capel Dewi, Llandysul SA44 4PS.
Telephone: Tony or Jennie on 01545 590376

Pantybedw Fishery

A 7.5-acre (barbless) catch-and-release lake and a 1.5-acre catch-and-keep lake.
Address: Pantybedw Fishery, Nantgaredig, Carmarthen SA32 7LH
Telephone: 01267 290315

Glynderwen Fishery

A 2.2 acre lake suitable for disabled anglers. Rainbow trout.
Address: Glynderwen, Llanwnnen, Lampeter SA48 7LS
Telephone: T W Morgans on 01570 434248

Nine Oaks Trout Pools

Four trout pools stocked with rainbow trout, plus a coarse fishery.
Address: Nine Oaks Trout Pools, Oakford, Llanarth, Nr New Quay SA47 0RW
Telephone: 01545 580482

Rhydlewis Fishery

A quiet 3-acre trout pool and smokery.
Address: Rhydlewis Fishery, Nr Rhydlewis, Llandysul SA55 5QS
Telephone: 01239 851224

Teifi Pools and Llyn Berwen

Six upland lakes controlled by Tregaron Angling Association.
Address: Brynteifi, Pont Llanio, Tregaron, Ceredigion SY25 6PS.
Telephone: Toby Jackson (Membership Secretary) on 01974 831316

Pant Trout Pool

A 10 acre pool; accepts caravans overnight if owner fishing.
Address: Pant Trout Pool, Llandewi Brefi, Tregaron, Ceredigion, SY25 6UQ
Telephone: Evan Jones on 01974 298753

Llys-y-fran and Rosebush Reservoirs

Approx. 200-acre rainbow trout reservoir and 50-acre wild brown trout reservoir.
Address: Llys-y-fran Country Park, Near Haverfordwest, Pembs SA63 4RS.
Telephone: 01437 532694

River Game Fisheries on the Teifi

Three large angling clubs control the majority of the fishing on the River Teifi, and they make a range of day, week and season permits available to local and visiting anglers. (Llandysul A A's fisheries on the Teifi are detailed in Chapter 2.) But there are also one or two smaller angling clubs with stretches of fishing, as well as a sprinkling of private fisheries that offer day or week permits, many of them linked to self-catering, B&B or hotel accommodation.

The bridge Pool, Pontllwni, a private fishery with self-catering cottages

Teifi Trout Association's fly-only fishing below Newcastle Emlyn Weir

Tregaron Angling Association

Approx. 22 miles of wild trout fishing on the upper Teifi; some salmon and sewin.
Address: Brynteifi, Pont Llanio, Llanddewi Brefi, Tregaron, Ceredigion.
Telephone: Toby Jackson (Membership Secretary), on 01974 831316

Llanybydder Angling Club

Approx. 5 miles of fishing, on the middle Teifi near Llanybydder.
Address: Dolau View, Neuadd Road, Llanybydder
Telephone: Andrew Morgan on 01570 480998 or 01570 480643

Pontllwni, Maesycrugiau

Approx. 1/2 mile of private fishing with self-contained riverside cottage.
Address: Pontllwni, Maes-y-crugiau, Pencader, Carmarthenshire.
Telephone: Velma Thomas SA39 9LT. Tel: 01559 395267.

County Gate Fishery

Approx. 1/2 mile on the right bank at Llanfihangel-ar-Arth, with B&B.
Address: County Gate, Llanfihangel-ar-Arth, Pencader, Carms SA39 9JB.
Telephone: Charles Gurman on 01559 395285

Faedr Fawr Fishery

Approx. 700 yards of right bank fishing and two self-catering cottages.
Address: Faedr Fawr, Llandysul, Ceredigion SA44 4PB.
Telephone: Mike Grayson on 01559 362177.

Dol Haidd Isaf

Approx. 3/4 mile, mainly single-bank at Pentrecagal; self-catering.
Address: Dol Haidd Isaf, Pentrecagal, Newcastle Emlyn, Carms SA38 9HU.
Telephone: Brian Scull on 01559 370084.

Teifi Trout Association

Approx. 20 miles of fishing on the lower Teifi.
Permits: tackle shops in Cardigan, Cilgerran and Cenarth.
Telephone Mike Evans (membership sec) on 01239 682767

Stradmore Gardens

Approx. 650 yards on the right bank two miles downstream of Cenarth.
Address: Stradmore Gardens, Cenarth, Newcastle Emlyn SA38 9LB.
Telephone: Irfon Davies on 01239 682417.

Castell Malgwyn Hotel

Approx. 1 mile of the left bank starting 300 yds downstream of Llechryd Bridge.
Address: Castell Malgwyn Hotel, Llechryd, Cardigan, SA43 2QA.
Telephone: 01239 682382.

Coarse Fisheries

Because there are so few coarse fish in the river, the Teifi itself has little to offer the coarse angler. In Tregaron Bog there are pike, but this is not a generally accessible fishery. Stoneloaches, bullheads, minnows and sticklebacks can be found throughout the river, but these species are of no significant interest from an angling point of view. Eels, while nowhere near as plentiful as they were twenty years ago, can still be caught on most of the slower reaches.

Rudd are stocked into many stillwater fisheries in the Teifi Valley

I don't want to give the impression that the Teifi Valey is a coarse-fishing desert; there are some very attractive and productive small stillwaters sprinkled around the area, and by any standards they offer good quality, accessible fishing at relatively low cost. Some of these stillwaters also have trout pools on the same site, and so all-round anglers can always hedge their bets.

One of the most striking of our freshwater fishes, the perch is the first species that many young anglers encounter.

Whether you opt for tackle simplicity or sophistication, coarse fishing can provide good sport all the year round at many of the stillwater fisheries in the Teifi Valley

Teglan Fishery

A carp lake and a match lake, both with excellent facilities for disabled anglers.
Address: Teglan Fishery, Ysbryd-y-Llyn, Ciliau Aeron, Lampeter, SA48 8DA
Telephone: David and Mark Owen on 01570 471115

Nine Oaks Fishery

A secluded coarse fishing lake. (Four trout fishing pools also on site.)
Address: Nine Oaks Fishery, Oakford, Near Aberaeron, Ceredigion SA47 0RW.
Telephone: 01545 580482

Yet y Gors Fishery

Two lakes stocked with carp, tench, bream and roach.
Address: Yet y Gors Fishery, Manorwen, Fishguard SA65 9RE.
Telephone: 01348 873497. Along Ferry Road, A4219 south of Fishguard.

Llanarth Fishery

Two-acre carp lake plus mixed coarse fish pond with access for disabled anglers.
Address: Llanarth Fishery, Ty'r Lon, Llanarth, Ceredigion, SA47 0NT.
Telephone: Nigel Pheysey on 01545 580598

Ian Heaps Premier Coarse Fisheries

Three lakes (total 90 pegs) stocked with carp to 24 lbs and tench to 6 lbs.
Address: Holgan Farm, Llawhaden, Narberth, Pembrokeshire SA67 8DJ.
Telephone: Ian Heaps on 01437 541285.

Carp specialists are catered for at most coarse fisheries in West Wales

Sea angling

The variety of sea fish around the Teifi Estuary is amazing. From the rocky shores anglers catch bass, bream, mullet, wrasse, conger, rockling, mullet and pollack as well as a few dogfish, smoothhhound, tope and even the occasional thornback ray.

Rays are caught from the beaches and rocky shores of West Wales

The storm beaches of Cardigan Bay face due west, and immediately after rough weather the bass fishing there can be particularly good. Shellfish are useful baits at such times, but sand-eels, ragworm, lobworm and strips of squid are also effective. Flatfish, whiting, mullet and dogfish are caught from the beaches in summer, while codling can give good winter sport.

Bass nursery areas

Bass spawn in estuaries around the coast of Wales, and in 1999 several such places were designated as bass nursery areas. Fishing for bass from a boat in these areas is prohibited during summer and autumn, as also is fishing with sand-eels as bait. Most shore anglers also return any bass they catch in these areas in order to contribute to conservation of this slow-growing but very valuable fish species.

Fishing from the rocky shores of Ceredigion

Whitesands Bay, one of the many wonderful Pembrokeshire beaches

The Teifi Estuary bass nursery area

In the Teifi Estuary, the waters enclosed by an imaginary line drawn from the boathouse at Penryn on the southern side to The Cliff Hotel on the northern side, are subject to bass nursery area restrictions throughout the months May to November inclusive. Other nursery areas in West Wales include Milford Haven, Bury Inlet and the combined estuary of the rivers Taf, Towy and Gwendraeth.

Dinghy launching sites

If you own a small boat, you can launch it using slipways at most ports including Aberystwyth, New Quay and St Dogmaels. Launching fees and harbour dues are payable in some locations, but use of the St Dogmaels slipway is free at present.

Charter boats

Charter boats operate from many ports around the coast of Wales, including Aberystwyth, New Quay and Milford Haven, which are within reasonable travelling distance of the Teifi Valley. Here I am including a selection of the charter boats that work out of ports near to the Teifi.

Milford Haven, homeport for several angling charter boats

All-day wreck and reef fishing trips are particularly popular in this area (and some skippers can provide night fishing trips too); however, for those with less stamina or too many other things to do each day, mackerel trips of just a couple of hours duration can provide fun for the family with every prospect of success.

Argo

> **Description**: Fast Lochin 333, range 60miles. Wreck fishing, mackerel etc.
> **Port**: Aberystwyth
> **Telephone**: D M Rees on 01545 560966

Aldebaran

> **Description**: C.O.P. to 60 miles; 11 anglers.
> **Port**: Aberystwyth
> **Telephone**: Dave Taylor on 01970 828815

Lady Jane

> **Description**: C.O.P. to 20 miles. Two to 12-hour trips.
> **Port**: Aberystwyth
> **Telephone**: Sean Roche on 01554 388492

Ma Chipe

> **Description**: C.O.P. to 60 miles.
> **Port**: Aberystwyth
> **Telephone**: 01970 623465

Swift

> **Description**: C.O.P. to 20 miles.
> **Port**: Aberystwyth
> **Telephone**: Nick Hughes on 01970 832536

Celtic Wildcat

> **Description**: Fast catamaran C.O.P. to 60 miles; 12 anglers.
> **Port**: Milford Haven
> **Telephone**: 1646 600313

Cleddau King

> **Description**: 40 ft Cygnus Cyfish; 400bhp Volvo Penta Engine. C.O.P. 60 miles.
> **Port**: Milford Haven
> **Telephone**: Alun Lewis on 01834 891222

Overdale

> **Description**: 38ft; twin-engine; 12 anglers.
> **Port**: Aberystwyth
> **Telephone**: Mr Chapman on 01437 767503

Sabre Tooth

> **Description**: Offshore 105; wreck and reef fishing trips.
> **Port**: Neyland
> **Telephone**: Phil or Steve on 01646 602672

CHAPTER 4
Flyfishing Tackle and Tactics

One of the things that make flyfishing so intriguing is the individuality of rivers. The nature of the terrain and its ecology; the underlying soil, rock, limestone or chalk; and the gradient of the watercourse - all of these features help determine the speed and chemical composition of the water and how these characteristics vary with time. Not surprisingly, the communities of creatures that live in a river evolve to suit that environment. Not only does the population density of each species adapt to suit the river but their age structure, size and even colouring and behaviour all become adapted to suit the ecology in which they live.

The tranquillity of the Teifi as it drifts past meadows and woodland in its middle reaches belies the rugged nature of its upper reaches

The Teifi is no exception. Over the ten thousand years since the end of the last Ice Age, the wild trout of the Teifi have evolved via two very different life strategies. Having first entered the river via the sea, some continue to make use of the rich feeding available in coastal waters around our shores, travelling just a few tens of miles from the river estuary before returning to find partners and reproduce. These sea trout look and behave very differently from their genetically very similar brethren the resident brown trout, which are slower growing and feed and breed within the freshwater confines of the river.

Terrestrial insects, such as these hawthorn flies, are much more important on some stretches of the Teifi than on others

Less tolerant of moving shadows and heavy footfalls than the larger wild trout that once populated the chalkstreams of southern England, Teifi brownies cannot afford to be quite so choosy about their food - but that does not make them easy to catch. Fool a Teifi pounder and you have every right to feel a sense of achievement.

Once they enter their natal rivers, sea trout are shy and easily spooked fish, and those that run the Teifi are no exceptions. The uniqueness of Teifi sewin lies in two features of their population: their abundance – some 20,000 sea trout run the Teifi in a typical year – and their very rapid growth rate combined with a potential for longevity. What this means is that provided they do not get killed by predators (and that includes anglers, of course) Teifi sea trout can put on two or three pounds in weight each winter that they spend in the sea, and they can survive to spawn many times. Some fish will run the Teifi every year for up to ten successive seasons - occasionally even more – and that is why a few lucky (and, it should be admitted, skilful) anglers encounter the occasional 15lb to 20lb monster sewin.

Salmon, too, evolve into strains suited to the river of their birth. Teifi salmon of a particular weight tend to be a little shorter than average and deeper in the belly. Some have suggested that this feature is the result of a natural selection process favouring those salmon with the muscle power necessary to leap the many waterfalls that punctuate their passage up the River Teifi. Certainly, Teifi salmon are powerful fighters, and this is an added attraction of our river as far as anglers are concerned.

And so to the fishing… In this chapter you will find suggestions for tackle set-ups, flies and fishing tactics that should at least help you get started on the Teifi with a reasonable prospect of catching trout, sea trout and salmon. Aware that despite its modest size the River Teifi can be a very challenging river, and the fish themselves certainly no pushovers, experienced Teifi anglers may like to experiment with some the more advanced tackle set-ups and flyfishing tactics outlined here.

Trout fishing

The average adult wild brown trout of the River Teifi grows to about ¾ lb in weight. Most of the fish that we catch are a lot smaller, of course, and that's mainly because there are a lot of small fish and only a few big ones. Out of 500 to 1000 eggs laid by a spawning trout, only one or two will survive to maturity. Many are eaten by predators before they even reach the parr stage, and although it is tempting to suggest that the survivors are the canniest and toughest of the brood it's probably more accurate to say that this is a matter of survival not of the fittest but of the most cowardly. Remembering always that fear is the number one motivator of a trout, and that the need to feed is secondary, can help us to focus on those factors that are most critical to flyfishing success.

A lovely wild brown trout being returned carefully to the river

Occasionally some very big brown trout feature in angling catches on the Teifi. The biggest fish I know of was a twelve pounder; however, this was a 'slob trout', an estuary-dwelling fish that had just managed to fight its seagoing tendencies. Another splendid specimen, caught in the mid 1990s from Pwll Artie on Llandysul A A's Penbeili beat, weighed a creditable 5 lb 4 oz. Fish of between two and three pounds in weight are caught almost every year, and in most cases they are taken by people fishing for sea trout in fast water as darkness is descending.

Tackle for wild brown trout

If you are new to trout fishing on rivers, you might well be able to use your existing stillwater trout tackle. Anything but the heaviest of stillwater gear will do at a push; however, because of the shyness of wild Teifi brown trout lightweight tackle has many advantages. Not only is the casting disturbance (the splash!) minimised by using a light line, but you can also use a finer leader without too great a risk of breakage whenever you tighten into a fish. If you are kitting up from scratch a balanced, lightweight outfit of the type listed below should be just about ideal:

Rod	8' 6" to 9' 6" middle-to-tip action with an AFTM rating of 5 or 6.
Reel	Any kind of fly-reel will do provided that it can accommodate the line and at least 50 yds of backing. Apart from ensuring that the spool is filled to the correct level, the backing will give you at least some chance with a salmon or a sea trout that ignores the 'trout only' rule!
Lines	A weight-forward floater matched to the rod will enable you to shoot line when you need to make a long cast. A double-taper floating line would do, of course, and has the advantage that it can be reversed on the reel should the leading taper get damaged; however, it is not so good when you need to cover a fish rising on the far side of a very wide pool.
Leaders	A three-foot butt section of around 20 lb breaking strain, to which you attach either a factory-made tapered leader or a stepped leader. The tippet must be fine when fishing calm water; nylon of 3lb breaking strain is often as coarse as you can get away with.
Accessories	Eye protection; a wading staff and a buoyancy aid or life preserver if you intend getting in to deep and/or fast water; and a landing net (if you use a net at all) with knotless mesh.
Dry Flies	See the section below on 'Matching the Hatch'.
Wet Flies	You can't go far wrong with March Brown, Greenwell's Glory, Coch-y-Bonddu, Blue Dun, Black Gnat, William's Favourite, Snipe & Purple, Waterhen Bloa, and Connemara Black.
Nymphs	Gold-ribbed Hare's Ear and Pheasant Tail Nymph will do fine.

Tactics for wild brown trout

Being a rain-fed (spate) river, the Teifi is subject to frequent fluctuations in height, colour, flow and temperature; all of these factors affect the fishing and should, therefore, influence how and where you fish on the river.

First find your fish

Beginners to wild trout fishing will find it is best to avoid the calm, slow stretches, where casting accuracy and presentation of the fly are most critical. Instead, concentrate on the with fast-flowing 'riffles' and the necks and tails of pools, where turbulence limits the fish's vision and helps to mask the presence of an angler. These are places where you can even get away with the occasional splashy cast. Other good places to try are the food lanes, which can easily be identified by looking for lines of bubbles or scum on the surface of the water. Back eddies where food and bubbles collected and drift in circles can also be productive.

Look out for places with good natural cover offering protection to the fish from their many predators such as herons and other fish-eating birds. These kinds of places are always worth a try, although acquiring the skill necessary to cast under low-hanging branches and bushes on the far side of the stream does take time. Remember that on calm stretches of water the first cast is nearly always your best chance – and sometimes your only chance - of catching a fish.

A classic hotspot: here a trout can lie beside a food lane in the shade of an overhanging bush, whose roots provide the perfect bolthole.

When fishing on clear rivers, how you dress and the way you move can be of great importance. To stand upright, clothed in bright colours, or even to approach the riverbank too quickly, can invite disaster. Ideally, what you wear, and most definitely your behaviour, should harmonize with the surroundings. In these circumstances it is also advisable to keep low down if wading or to crouch or kneel when fishing from the bank. Shadows falling suddenly upon the stream will also send wild fish scurrying for cover. Try to fish from a position that keeps your shadow off the water. If this is not possible, kneel down to minimise your shadow. High-gloss rods and reels can also reflect the sun and scare trout, as can brightly coloured fly lines glinting against a dark background.

Matching the hatch

Wild trout of the Teifi are not spoilt, and most of the time they are only too pleased to see a fly of any sort; however, they don't simply grab at any old offering. Drag – where a dry fly skates due to turbulent surface currents pulling on the leader – will deter all but the tiddlers. Similarly, they are wary of too heavy a leader, or of a leader tippet that is greasy and floats high up on the surface, creating a meniscus whose shadow is much wider than the leader itself. Provided you can avoid these obvious giveaways, getting the size and general form of the fly to match the flies of the season is often quite sufficient. Thankfully (for the sale of books on angling entomology, at least!) there are still a few hatches that are so prolific that a good match makes quite a difference to the prospects of catching trout on the Teifi. Some of the most important of these are summarised below:

March Brown

This large, mottled brown fly hatches from the third week in March into the second week of April. The timing does not alter much from year to year but the density of the hatch certainly does. In a good year the hatch on some stretches is so prolific that the fish go mad… but you have to be there at the right time of day, and that is rather less repeatable from season to season. Rarely do the first March Brown duns appear before about 11a.m. and the excitement is over by about 3 p.m. Often these flies come off in waves over a period of 10 to 15 minutes, with very few thereafter until perhaps an hour or so later when there is another burst of activity. By early April there may be three or four such feeding bursts; alternatively we can get such a big spate that by the time the river is fishable the March Browns are long gone.

Grannom

The Grannom sedge is the most reliable of all Teifi hatches. From mid April until early May get to the river before 10am. By 11am the air is still full of sedge flies but the rises are few, because these little fawn early risers are such good fliers that very few get blown on to the surface. The message from all this is a clear one: fish a small sedge pupa or sedge emerger imitation early in the morning, after which you might just as well use a Large Dark Olive imitator such as Kite's Imperial.

Hawthorn Fly

Black gnats of many kinds are important sources of food for trout, and on the upper and middle Teifi the most important of these is the Hawthorn Fly, an insect of terrestrial origin that gets blown onto the water on breezy days. A Coch-y-Bonddu will do as a general imitation, but when the hatch is at its peak in early May it's worth having a closer imitation.

Hawthorn Fly designed and tied by Jon Beer

Yellow May

From early June through to mid August the Yellow May duns emerge in late afternoon and early evening. As big as a March Brown and just a welcome to a hungry trout, this fly really can cause a selective rise, especially as the egg-laying spinner comes down to the surface quite early in the evening and adds to the feeding bonanza. On warm and calm evenings trout sometimes become totally preoccupied with these golden beauties, and then a bright yellow artificial fly is almost essential to success.

Mike Weaver's Sparkle Dun is very effective when trout are taking Yellow Mays in either their dun or spinner stage.

Olives

All of the *Baëtis* olive duns of summer – the Medium Olive, Small Dark Olive, Pale Watery, both spurwings and even the Iron Blue - can be copied adequately with a general-purpose dun imitation of the appropriate size (14 or 16). A Greenwell's Glory or a Rough Olive work very well, I find.

Blue-winged Olive

Although different in behaviour and habitat, the Blue-winged Olive, still a very important summer fly on the Teifi, is also matched adequately in the dun stage by a Greenwell's. A Sherry Spinner, preferably tied with its wings in the spent position, is perfect for the early evening spinner rise.

A spent-winged Sherry Spinner for the early evening rise on warm summer evenings

Sandfly and Caperer

These two orange-brown sedge flies are plentiful on most beats and contribute in no small way to the late-evening rise. You really need a warm muggy evening for best results; in contrast, a chill mist kills the flies before they can return to lay their eggs, and this puts an early end to dry fly fishing. A good imitation of the Sandfly is the orange G & H Sedge, a deer-hair pattern devised by John Goddard and the late Cliff Henry; tie it small (size 12 maximum) for best results to mimic the Sandfly, and size 10 when Caperers are more in evidence.

Seen from beneath the surface of the water, this Deveaux Sedge is a very good imitation of a spent sedge fly; It works best if fished either static in a backwater eddy or twitched periodically as it drifts on a gentle current.

Although they have been scarce in recent years, every now and then we get a good Mayfly season on the Teifi, and then a close imitation will outperform a general-purpose pattern such as Grey Wulff.

Sea trout fishing

Virtually every year the Teifi secures either first or second place in the league of sea trout rivers in England and Wales, ranked by total rod catch. (In 2001, 2002 and again in 2003 the Teifi took the number one position, for example.) In a good year the Teifi rod catch can exceed 4000, while around 2500 is perhaps more typical. Most of them are small fish, and it is tempting to assume that the reason for this is that the run comprises mainly small fish. Not so. The average size of the sea trout that we catch is determined more by how we fish than by anything else, and it may come as little surprise that the biggest sea trout tend to inhabit the deep, well shaded water that is the most difficult to fish effectively.

Summer sea trout fishing

In this section, I will suggest ways in which newcomers to sea trout fishing can increase their chances of catching at least a few fish in their first season, while for the more experienced flyfisher I'll be proposing more challenging tackle set-ups, techniques and tactics that can significantly increase the chance of making contact with one of those monster sea trout for which the Teifi and its neighbouring West Wales rivers Towy and Rheidol (to name just two of several) are so famous. Fish of 10 lb, 15 lb and even 20 lb run our river, but be warned: they do not grow as big as that by being easy to catch!

Tackling up for sea trout

There is no need to go to huge expense when tackling up for night fishing for sewin. Most stillwater or river trout tackle (other than lightweight brook rods) will do the job reasonably well; however, if you are kitting up from scratch you might like to know about the sort of equipment that many local anglers find serves them well:

Rod	9' 6" to 10' 6" with an AFTM rating of 7 or 8. The action should not be too fast. (A stiff rod with a very short flexible length of top joint will not absorb the shock of a leaping sea trout.)
Reel	Any reliable trout fly-reel will do provided that it can accommodate the line and at least 50 yds of backing. Large arbour reels are becoming increasingly popular because of their ability to gather in line quickly should it be necessary to follow a powerful running fish.
Lines	Floater, intermediate, and fast sink. You will probably make most use of the floater in the summer months, so go for this type if you only buy one line. Double taper lines are preferred by some sea trout fishers because they find that the thin running line of a weight forward is harder to see in the dark. Whichever you choose, a white line is more visible at night, when movement of the line can serve as a useful 'take' indication.
Leaders	A three-foot butt section of around 25 lb breaking strain plus approximately nine feet of 10 lb breaking strain nylon should be about right for fishing small flies early in the evening. Larger flies demand shorter, stronger leaders – for example when using a large, aluminium-bodied tube fly just a couple of feet of 15 lb nylon attached to the three-foot butt should be adequate. Check your leader periodically for wind knots, which can seriously weaken the nylon.
Accessories	Eye protection; a wading staff and a buoyancy aid or life preserver if you intend getting in to deep and/or fast water; a stout landing net (if you use a net at all) with knotless mesh, and a priest. A reliable torch is also essential for night fishing.
Flies	Butcher, Alexandra, Haslam, Dunkeld, Dark Mackerel and Sweeny Todd are all popular patterns that can work well in clear water. Silver Doctor, Medicine and Teifi Terror can be remarkably effective when there is a hint of colour in the water. The main thing is to have a range of sizes, from single-hook size 12s right up to three-inch weighted tube flies or waddington lures, to suit various states of the river, times of night and levels of light. Surface Lures and even Deer-hair Sedge patterns can also tempt fish if dragged across the surface to create a wake beneath overhanging trees or on a flat-calm pool.

The importance of confidence

Having confidence in your chosen fly is really important: it helps you to concentrate so that you remain alert enough to react to a take before the sea trout 'lets go'.

If you are new to sea trout fishing and find the above list of flies confusing, here are three flies that will bring sea trout to your net over a range of river conditions:

- Teal, Blue & Silver, sizes 8, 6 and 4
- Butcher, sizes. 10, 8 and 6
- Mallard & Claret, sizes 12, 10 and 8

Rod Licence

Note that you will need a 'Salmon' licence if you are going to fish for sea trout; a 'Trout/Coarse' fishing licence will not do.

Safety precautions

In chapter 7 there is a Fact File on the subject of fishing safety, but a few key points deserve emphasis here. Fishing for sea trout at night presents extra hazards over and above those of daytime fishing, and so some of the precautions we can take are worth restating.

- If you intend to wade during the night, visit the spot during daylight hours and make yourself familiar with that particular stretch of water.
- If you are going fishing alone then let someone know where you intend to fish and what time you expect to be back.
- When casting flies in the dark, a leaf or tiny bit of weed attached to the fly may be all that's needed to ruin what would have been a good back cast. If you don't wear eye protection the first inkling you may get that something is wrong is when a fly hits your eye.

The role of a sea trout fly

With one special exception – wake fly tactics, which I will cover later – the methods of fishing for sea trout have much in common with those used to catch wild brown trout on rivers and lakes. The big difference, however, is that we are not trying to use our artificial fly to mimic the appearance and behaviour of insects upon which the fish are feeding; instead, we are merely trying to lure the sea trout into grabbing hold of our fly, whether it be out of curiosity, aggressive protection of its chosen territory (its 'lie'), or simply an instinctive reaction to seeing food-like movement and form (even though, like its cousin the salmon, a sea trout does not need to feed when in freshwater).

Wet flies

Most of the sea trout that are caught by flyfishers – and nearly all of the very big ones for which the West Wales rivers are renowned – fall to moving flies fished below the surface rather than to dry flies floating along on the current. For that reason, if you are new to this challenging branch of the sport I would urge you to concentrate on fishing with a small selection of wet flies in a wide range of sizes.

Dry flies

There are times when small sea trout - in particular whitling that have been to sea for just a few months before returning to the river - will take a dry fly, even during the day. This method works best in shaded reaches of the river. It is not a technique recommended for early in the year when most of the larger sea trout run, but it comes into its own as the season advances. Dry fly fishing can be very effective as the water fines off following an autumn spate; at such times olive dun imitations, such as Rough Olive or Greenwell's Glory in sizes 14 and 16, are worth a try.

A general representation 'dun' such as Greenwell's Glory will tempt whitling as an autumn spate is fining down

The influence of weather

For the best of fishing with the fly, the night needs to be warm and overcast and the river at a moderate or low level. Then a floating or intermediate line would normally be used, at least in the early part of the night. Changeable weather, especially when the river is running high or the air temperature is much colder than that of the water, may require you to use a sinking line; in these conditions larger and brighter flies tend to be more effective provided they are retrieved slowly near the riverbed.

Where and when to start

Except when the river is high or coloured, it usually pays to wait for nightfall before beginning to fish, otherwise you are likely to disturb the sea trout. It is also a good idea to rest your water periodically, for ten minutes or so, during the night. The tail of a pool is usually a productive spot as fish drop back to this position after dusk. Later in the night, potential lies on the whole of the pool are worth searching methodically. Sea trout often rest against the bank beneath overhanging trees, so search these kinds of places particularly thoroughly. Sooner or later you will encounter a shoal of sea trout, and the action will start.

Sea Trout Tactics

Regardless of which fly patterns you use, you will need to select flies according to the prevailing fishing conditions. Many anglers would agree that the actual fly pattern is not such an important factor, but fly size, weight, shape and durability certainly do matter.

At dusk, a small fly will catch sea trout when a larger fly may even spook them. Bright moonlit nights also call for smaller flies – size 12 or even 14 may be necessary, but they really *must* be tied on strong forged hooks.

Butcher: a durable and well-proven catcher of sea trout

On cloudy or moonless nights sea trout may fail to see and react to very small flies, and then something larger is necessary. Similarly, when fishing deep water late at night even a three-inch tube fly or Waddington lure is not too big. Throughout most of the season, big flies fished in the deepest places do tend to catch more of the very big sea trout.

Running fish

When the sea trout are running, concentrate on the run line – the route the fish take when moving through a pool. If your fly passes across the nose of a running fish it is likely to be taken; the run line is where this will happen. Being able to find the run line is therefore a useful skill, and here are some clues to doing so:

- Concentrate on the region two to six yards above the point where the water begins breaking up at the tail of a pool, and in particular just above any downstream-pointing vee that marks the greatest current concentration.
- In the belly or dub of the pool, the current concentration (and hence the run line) is usually close to the surface foam line (unless a crosswind is sweeping any foam to one side).
- Sea trout about to leave the pool often surface where a vee of turbulent water extends into the calmer water at the neck of a pool. Drift a fly slowly across the current there, and be prepared for a violent take as the fish turns in fast water.

Resting fish

Resters are sea trout that have been in the river for several weeks. Resting sea trout can be harder to find, and they are more likely to swim behind a fly, nipping at it tentatively so that all you see or feel is just the slightest of taps on the line. Hugh Falkus devised his Secret Weapon fly, with a flying treble hook tied in behind the main, dressed hook, to deal these difficult sea trout. When nipping fish 'take short' so that they do not engulf the main hook, they still get caught on the flying treble. Because of this tendency of resting sea trout to 'take short', as it is called, summer sea trout flies are often tied with little or no tail or wing material extending behind the bend of the hook.

Secret Weapon

When they stop running and settle into a pool, sea trout do not spread out evenly, and in fact most of the water is not even worth casting into. You may get takes in midstream, but don't be fooled: any fish that you catch there are likely to have left their bank-side lies and to have followed your fly for quite some distance. Concentrate on casting right into their lies, which are nearly always hard against the riverbank or against a substantial submerged object such as a rock ledge or a sunken tree stump.

So what *do* you have to do to get a sea trout to take your fly? In many instances, dropping a fly onto the surface directly above a sea trout that is resting in shallow water and then moving the fly away can be quite enough to provoke a take. Sea trout in very deep water are not so easily caught, however, unless the fly is also presented at the right depth. Sink tips and sinking lines will provide you with the all-important facility of depth control.

Sea trout lies

In the (sea trout) housing market, location is everything. The most important factor of all, therefore, is to get your fly right into the sea trout's lie. To do this you need to hone your skills until you can cast accurately and turn your leader over properly - not just in the daylight but, crucially, in the dark! Seasoned sea trout fishers sometimes use two or three flies at a time in the belief that it increases their chance of success. In some circumstances I am sure it does... but the increase is certainly not a factor of two or three times or anything like that. Don't be over ambitious, therefore: one fly cast well is much better than a team of flies landing in a tangle.

In general, the best sea trout lies are on the deeper side of the river, hard against the bank; that is where most of the fish spend the daylight hours, heads tucked beneath undercuts or into dense tangles of tree roots. The ability to cast your flies into the lies but not into the trees is something that comes only with practice.

Casting from the shallow side of a pool into deep, dark water

Matching the set-up to the situation

Early in the evening (and throughout a moonlit night) you are likely to need a long leader in order to keep the very visible fly line well clear of the area you are fishing. This is all the more important when the river is low, slow, clear and calm. But there really is no need for long leaders when casting heavy flies and a sinking line in the dead of a dark night – in fact a long leader could even reduce the rate of descent of your fly so that it never gets down to where the fish are resting. In low light conditions, six feet of leader may be more than enough - and a short leader makes the casting much so more manageable, especially when you are wading in a tree-lined river where continuous motions casts (Spey casts and snake roll casts, for example) are necessary.

Don't get stuck in a rut – unless you are catching fish, of course. If the sea trout are not taking your offering, you need to change something. It is tempting to change fly pattern, but that rarely seems to make much difference. Instead, change the depth at which you work the fly through the water, or vary its size, until you do get a response; but at all times ensure that your fly does not simply drift lifelessly, like just another bit of waterlogged debris carried along on the current. Fish see lots of debris drifting part, and they are unlikely to react to one more such spectre.

Another important variable is the way that your fly moves through the water. For example, if a long line cast so that the fly swings slowly out from far bank into a mainstream position fails to provoke a sea trout into taking your fly, try shortening the line and casting straight across the current, working the fly rapidly and jerkily. This technique most often induces takes early in the evening.

You are not limited to across and downstream fishing, of course. Another option, which is sometimes very effective when fish are lying deep down in rock gullies, is to cast *upstream* and across. In this way you can let the fly sink as it drifts towards a suspected lie and then lift the rod tip so that you bring the fly alive to 'induce' a take (just as a nymph fisher might do when trout fishing). This upstream tactic can be deadly on bright moonlit nights when sea trout are more easily spooked by a fly that is cast straight into their lies.

Waking them up with a wake fly

There are summer nights when you could easily be convinced that every sea trout that had run the river had had second thoughts and gone back to sea. When no sea trout leap and splash on the surface, try dragging a wake fly across the calmest, deepest parts of a pool. The fish are there, but it is as if they had been nailed to the riverbed. A surface disturbance is sometimes all you need to get them moving. Often you can wake up these lethargic sea trout using flies made from cork or balsa wood; an alternative is to use a short-tailed Muddler Minnow. Anything that floats will do - even a strip of Ethafoam tied on to the top of a bare hook.

This Surface Lure relies on the natural buoyancy of deer hair fibres, which are hollow and so trap air within the fly

Salmon Fishing

Despite the decline in salmon stocks on most rivers in the British Isles, the Teifi still has a pretty good reputation as a salmon river. The spring run is less prolific than it was some forty years ago, and the majority of salmon are now caught in late summer and autumn. Gone are the portmanteau multi-sea-winter fish, the thirty pounders, quite a number of which appeared in catch statistics almost every year. Nevertheless, in a good season between 100 and 200 spring salmon are still caught on the Teifi out of a total catch of around 600 and occasionally over 1000. Low flows can make a very big difference, of course, and in a drought year the total salmon catch may be a mere 300 or so. That is the nature of salmon fishing, as indeed it has always been.

Casting skill is just one of the keys to successful salmon fishing

Success with salmon depends upon a combination of skill, knowledge and that other vital ingredient: luck. If you live a long way from the Teifi, you might come fishing unaware that the river is either a raging torrent or a pathetic trickle, and in that sense at least you would be very lucky indeed to catch a salmon. You can easily fix that one by checking the reading of the Teifi height gauge (telephone 0906 619 7755) or by calling a friend who lives locally before setting off. Some months are generally better than others, however, and past performance is a pretty good guide. In recent years the best spring fishing has been in May, while the grilse have been appearing rather late – early August is now usually better than mid July when the main grilse run generally began only a decade or two ago. The autumn run also comes later than it used to: the fishing rarely takes off until the second or even the third week of September – but so much depends upon the timing of the first real autumn spate.

Tackling up for salmon

A reasonably powerful single-handed reservoir rod (rated for a #8 line) makes quite a good salmon rod for all but the largest of pools on the Teifi and is certainly more than adequatre for grilse fishing; however, when the water level rises after heavy rain a double-handed rod makes it a lot easier to control the movement of the fly across the river: the extra length of the rod enables you to hold more of the line up off the surface. If you are tackling up from scratch it might be helpful to know what equipment local anglers generally use. For summer (grilse) fishing the sea trout outfit described on page 142 should be fine, while for spring and autumn fishing here is a typical high-water outfit well suited to the River Teifi:

Rod	13 ft double-handed rod rated for a #9 or #10 line. A rod longer than 14ft is more of a hindrance than a help on most Teifi beats, which are too narrow to justify such a long rod.
Lines	Floater (or intermediate) and fast sink double-taper. Unless the river is in spate, a floater with a super-fast sinking braided leader will generally do well in all but the deepest of pools; such a set-up is easier to cast than a conventional sink-tip line. Have at least 50yds of 25lb breaking strain backing, and preferably more... just in case.
Leaders	A 3 ft butt section of around 25 lb breaking strain plus 12 ft of tapered salmon leader to 8 lb breaking strain for low water fishing; fast-sinking polytips or tapered sinking braids plus 4 ft of level 12 to 15 lb nylon for spring and autumn fishing.
Accessories	Eye protection; a wading staff and a buoyancy aid or life preserver if you intend getting in to deep and/or fast water; a large, stout landing net (if you use a net at all) with knotless mesh (the use of tailers and gaffs is not permitted), and a priest if you intend killing any salmon.
Flies	Two flies that have increased in popularity on the Teifi in recent years are Ally's Shrimp, which shows up well and can be deadly in coloured water; and Stoat's Tail, a dark pattern that seems to be particularly effective when fishing for shy salmon in clear water. You will need them in a range of hook sizes. (See the section that follows on the subject of 'Salmon fishing tactics'.)

Salmon fishing tactics

Salmon travel up river in short bursts with periods of resting in between. While there is no evidence that running fish are less likely to take a fly than resting fish, what is quite clear is that the chances of a running fish seeing your fly are much reduced. You may get several chances to cast to a resting fish, but a runner can easily pass you between casts. Where the rules of the fishery require you to take a pace downstream between casts your prospect of catching any particular running fish are even further reduced; conversely, if the rules allow (or in some instances require) a pace upstream between casts there is an increased chance that any particular running fish will see your fly.

Most fish run well below the surface - often very close to the riverbed - and it helps if you can present your fly at or close to the depth the salmon are running. Sink-tips or full sinking lines may therefore be necessary on all but the shallowest sections of river.

Except when the water is very cold, resting salmon will swim up to take a fly, and therefore it is often possible to catch resters using a floating line and a fly presented just beneath the surface (and occasionally even a floating fly, although this is not a major tactic on rivers). The key to success is getting your fly to swim over the lies taken up by resting fish. But how do you find these lies?

Part of the enjoyment of fishing is learning to read the river for yourself, and so here are a few points that can help you to find fish even if you have no local expert to guide you:

- Spring salmon tend to rest in the depressions that occur upstream of or alongside submerged boulders. Such areas of 'broken ground' are most productive when there is a strong flow. Look for the surface turbulence caused by water upwelling as it flows over a boulder, but be aware that the visible evidence is always some distance downstream of the actual obstruction that causes the upwelling.

- After struggling up a stretch of fast water, salmon often rest for a short while as soon as they enter the calmer water of a pool. There is usually a good 'taking lie' on a pool tail a few yards upstream of the point where the water begins breaking as it enters the rapids between pool.

- In warm weather, grilse in particular favour the well-oxygenated water at the neck of a pool, and on summer evenings a fly drifted across the neck will often tempt a fish.

- On sunny days, fast-flowing glides that are overhung by trees provide a shady respite for salmon that are working their way steadily up river. Fish tend to rest there during the heat of the day before continuing their upstream migration during the hours of dusk and darkness. Provided you move slowly, the turbulent nature of such streamy and perhaps weedy water can help you to get closer to the fish without being seen. Gentle casting, using a long leader, is necessary; otherwise the salmon are likely to make an explosive dash away from your fly rather than being tempted to take it.

Shadows on the stream

On bright days the moving shadow that a floating line casts on the riverbed can startle fish. An intermediate line casts a much thinner shadow that a full floater. At such times it is also advisable to use a long leader (12 to 15 ft may be necessary) to keep the fly well away from the fly line and its shadow.

Fly sizes and patterns

You will need only a small selection of fly patterns, but do vary the size according to water height, temperature and clarity. When fishing deep water a larger fly usually works better than a small one, and in low light conditions or when visibility is limited by water turbidity a salmon may not see your fly at all if it is too small. On the other hand, bright summer days call for small flies; indeed, too big a fly can even spook the fish in low, clear water.

Ally's Shrimp

Working the fly

It's not just line density that sets the depth; the size and weight of the fly also affect the rate at which it sinks. A sparsely dressed fly of a given size and weight will sink faster than a heavily dressed one, just as fine leaders cut through the water more quickly than thicker ones. Where you cast your fly also affects the rate of sinking. If you cast across the river at right angles to the flow, the current will bring your fly more quickly towards your bank than if you cast at an oblique angle downstream. And if you cast upstream and across the fly will initially sink with minimal drag before it begins swimming across the river. By varying these factors you can control of the depth, the speed at which your fly travels, and the angle of presentation across the nose of a salmon. Finding the right combination of depth, presentation angle and speed can be crucial to triggering a response from the salmon.

You can also control how your fly moves through the water. Salmon that have seen lots of debris drifting by are unlikely to grab everything the passes their noses. Many salmon fishers say that giving the line a series of short pulls to make the fly behave like a living creature increases their catch rate. There could be something in this: the most successful salmon fishers are more than just good casters.

Safety reminder

If you are going salmon fishing alone, inform someone of where you intend to fish - especially when the river is in spate. It's a good idea to let them know what time you expect to be back. A modern buoyancy aid of the self-inflating type has the advantage of being less bulky than a conventional 'life jacket' or foam-lined waistcoat. This kind of investment has a high price tag, but it could save your life.

Catch and release

Releasing at least some of the fish that you catch is a legal requirement. If you catch parr, smolts or adult fish below a specified size you must release them with the minimum of delay. Kelts, baggots, and 'coloured' fish that are close to spawning must also be returned to the river. Some of the coloured salmon caught in autumn are spring-run fish that have spent several months in the river, and the early-running multi-sea-winter component of salmon stocks has suffered most severely from reduced survival during their time out at sea. Releasing these salmon to spawn is particularly important, therefore, for the future of the river.

 Since 1999 throughout England and Wales it has been a statutory requirement that all salmon caught by anglers before 16th June must also be released. The depleted state of wild Atlantic salmon stocks has also prompted an increase in 'voluntary catch and release'. The main problem may not be angling exploitation, but until stocks recover anglers can avoid making things worse by not taking home more than the occasional salmon as a special treat.

Catch and release: is it really worthwhile?

Some people ask what evidence there is that catch and release achieves anything. Do salmon (in particular, but equally wild brown trout and those very precious large sea trout) that are caught by flyfishers and then released survive to spawn?

Stale cock salmon such as this one are of far more value to the future stock of the river than they are as food for the angler who catches them

The survival rate depends upon water temperature and on how the salmon are handled. Not surprisingly, salmon caught when the water is warm and low in dissolved oxygen can cope with less stress than fish caught when the water is cold. Research shows that if the tackle used is strong enough to allow salmon to be brought in quickly rather than being played to exhaustion, and if the fish are handled correctly during unhooking and released without undue delay, around 85 per cent of spring salmon will survive to spawn, and an even higher survival rate can be expected of autumn fish. Given that while in the river some 15 per cent of salmon die of natural causes (predation, disease or injuries suffered when leaping rocky waterfalls, for example) the inference is that angling losses can usually be reduced to an insignificant level.

Best practice guidelines for handling and releasing fish
Following these simple guidelines will ensure that the salmon, trout and sea trout that you catch and release stand maximum chance of surviving to spawn and contribute to healthy Teifi fish stocks for the future:
- Fish with single hooks, either barbless or with the barbs squeezed down
- Use tackle strong enough to subdue the fish quickly
- If possible, keep the fish in the water while unhooking it
- If tasking a photograph, hold the fish horizontally, not vertically by the tail
- Don't waste time weighing a fish that you intend returning to the river; instead, simply measure its length against your fishing rod
- When releasing a fish, hold it in the current with its head facing upstream until it is ready and able to swim away unaided

A spring salmon being returned to the river

CHAPTER 5
Ecology and Wildlife of the Teifi Valley

For anyone interested in scenic beauty, ecology and wildlife diversity the Teifi Valley is truly wonderful. Not surprisingly, most anglers who fish in such wild places get a lot of extra pleasure from their days at the waterside just *because* there is so much to be seen and marvelled at. The majority of Llandysul A A members live a long way from the valley - indeed more than fifty per cent of members and by far the majority of short-term holiday visitors to the club's waters come from outside Wales - and that includes quite a few people from mainland Europe as well as Canada, the USA and the Far East to visit our fisheries on the Teifi Valley. So, whether you live in or are a visitor to the Teifi Valley, I hope that the next few pages will give you a taste of what this part of Wales has to offer.

Scenic beauty

Summer on the Teifi at Cwmmackwith

In Chapter 2 there are pictures taken at each of Llandysul A A's fishing beats on the Teifi, and I think they illustrate very well the scenic diversity of the river. In this chapter, therefore, the focus is on some of the many kinds of plants and animals that you are likely to come across during your travels in the valley.

Wildflowers

Within the river, beside the river, in the hedgerows and hillsides overlooking the river – all these are locations where a vast range of wildflowers can be seen, and in some places they are still so abundant as to provide quite breathtaking displays in spring, summer and autumn. Indeed, if you are interested in trees, then winter in the Teifi Valley also has much to offer.

Ranunculus, or Water Crowfoot, an aquatic buttercup species pictured here in bloom in June

A Flyfisher's Guide to the Teifi Valley

On many of the sunlit shallow stretches of the river – the pool tails and the glides – Ranunculus, or Water Crowfoot as this aquatic member of the buttercup family is commonly known – provides a sparkling display from late spring until the end of summer. Its rich beds of Ranunculus are among the reasons that the Teifi is designated a candidate Special Area of Conservation (cSAC). The latter is a European designation for sites of major conservation importance. *Ranculus pseudofluitans,* not a particularly rare species, is plentiful on the Teifi, but other quite rare species of Ranunculus also occur in the valley.

Bluebells in the Teifi Valley

Snowdrops, violets, wild daffodils, primroses, cowslips, lesser celandines, bluebells, wood sorrel, wild garlic and wood anemones add colour to a walk on the wild side. In the margins of the river look out for branched burr reed, purple loosestrife (not as widespread as it used to be), yellow loosestrife, water mint and that most splendid of all the buttercups, the Marsh Marigold.

Marsh Marigolds beside the Teifi at Hendy

On the cliff tops around the Teifi Estuary you can find the lovely Spring Squill

In shady hollows, you may also find the Three-cornered Leek

In the upper reaches of the Teifi catchment, Bog Asphodel bloom in summer.

A blanket of Bog Asphodel beside an upland tributary

Cornflowers still grow in a few waterside places in the Teifi Valley

Water Mint, Marsh Woundwort, Aquilegia, Ragged Robin, various Campions and Cranesbills add variety to the waterside scenery; they also provide essential habitat for insects and other creatures. You may still find Cornflowers in a few places.

Many of our marginal plants are now under threat. Himalayan Balsam, a beautiful but fiercely invasive alien plant brought to Britain in Victorian times has colonised large stretches of riverbanks. The upper and middle Teifi have largely been spared, but from Newcastle Emlyn downstream the banks are eight feet tall in summer with swathes of Himalayan balsam in places more than twenty feet deep. Regular cutting provides some control of these unwelcome introductions.

Himalayan Balsam – a beastly beauty

Talk of wild orchids in Britain and most people think of the chalk downland of southern England – and quite rightly, because so many species can be found there. But when you consider the diversity of soil types and substrates bordering the Teifi it may come as little surprise to hear that a great many wild orchids also occur here.

Bee Orchid

Greater Butterfly Orchid

Early Purple Orchid

Common Spotted Orchid

A Flyfisher's Guide to the Teifi Valley

In boggy parts of the Teifi Valley, bold stands of yellow Flag Iris make a pleasant change from the invasive Himalayan Balsam and Japanese Knotweed that have now taken over so much of Britain's riverbanks. Newly hatched fish fry escape predators by hiding among the stems of these emergent plants.

Flag Iris in the Teifi Valley

Hawthorn beside the upper Teifi

As autumn arrives, the tinge of sadness felt by anglers at the impending close of another season is tempered by the knowledge that the Teifi Valley is often at its most scenic as the leaves are turning and fruits are ripening.

Dry years bring the most colourful of falls. Fruits of the Rowan (mountain ash) turn from green to brightest orange; haws deepest red remain on leafless thorns; holly blushes faster than the birds can strip it of its berries; and the maples, scarce though they are in Wales, stand out from the crowd to make dull sycamore, ash and lime appear rank amateurs in the blush-of-the-month competition. Skeletal tree silhouettes punctuate a more open riverscape, and those with a mycologists' stoop turn their eyes downwards towards Natures's forgotten kingdom of fungi.

Fungi

It was with some trepidation that I first included fungi in the wildlife pages of Current Affairs, the newsletter of Llandysul Angling Association. Would anyone be interested? Would I be accused of wasting valuable space with irrelevancies? I need not have been concerned, it seems, for I have received more enquiries about fungi than any other wildlife topic covered in the forty or more editions of the newsletter that I have written since 1987. So for those who wonder at those strange, colourful and weirdly shaped organisms that spring up (literally overnight in some instances) here is just a tiny sample of the many thousands of species of fungi to be found in the fields, hedgerows and woodland beside the River Teifi.

Honey Fungus growing on a pine stump

Many of these fungi are not only edible but very much more tasty than the traditional button mushrooms that are all that many of us ever get to try. If you know how to identify them with certainty, then there are many more fungi worth collecting on your way back from a day on the river. Among the very best are Chanterelles, Ceps and Oyster Mushrooms – all now available at supermarkets (albeit at a high price). But have you ever tasted Hedgehog Mushrooms, Yellow Legs, St George's Mushrooms, Amethyst Deceivers? These and many more are considered great delicacies in countries where mycophiles scour fields and forests for free food. Know your mushrooms and you can enjoy free meals from January to December. Autumn, however, is the peak of the Teifi Valley fungus festival.

Chanterelle

Amethyst Deceiver

Cep, or Penny Bun Bolete

Hedgehog Mushroom

As everyone should know, some wild fungi are poisonous. It is hardly surprising that an area as rich in ecology as the Teifi Valley is home to many poisonous species. Reserve the label Toadstool for them if you will, but some of the most deadly of fungi are also among the most beautiful. Take for example (or should that be *under no circumstances take*?) the Death Cap, *Amanita phalloides*. This one species accounts for at least 80 per cent of the fatal fungus poisonings in the world; and it grows under oak trees here in Wales, as elsewhere in the British Isles.

Some Death Cap specimens are pale enough to be confused with Field Mushrooms - a mistake nobody makes twice.

To conclude this brief foray into a complex but intriguing subject, here are two more beautiful fungi that are common sights in the Teifi Valley.

Fly Agaric – *Amanita muscaria*

Scarlet Hood waxcaps – *Hygrocybe coccinea*

Insects

If you fish for wild trout, you will need to know quite a lot about the aquatic insects of rivers and lakes. The fly life of the Teifi Valley is discussed in some detail in Chapter 9, and so here we will look at just a few of the creatures that brighten a day's fishing. Let's begin with a group of four-winged insects that are of limited interest from a river fishing point of view but which are difficult to ignore on sunny summer days - dragonflies and damselflies, the kingfishers of the insect world.

**Common Blue Damselflies
mating in a 'damsel wheel'**

There are some forty or so species of dragonflies and damselflies in the British Isles, and many of them can be found in the Teifi catchment. The rare Southern Damsel can be found Preseli Hills, whereas the Common Blue Damsel is abundant on all shallow stillwaters and even occurs in some backwaters of the River Teifi itself.

A bronze-bodied river damselfly   **'Birth' of a Large Red Damselfly**

Dragonflies are more acrobatic than any helicopter. They can fly forwards, backwards and sideways, and they catch their food using nets – well, at least net-like structures formed from their six legs. Red, blue, green, yellow – dragonflies come in a rainbow of colours, brightening even the dullest of fishing days. They all have their favourite perches on vegetation overhanging the water, and it is to these spots that they return to munch their lunch of mayflies, midges, sedge flies and even the occasional damselfly. Find a little mound of insect wings, look up, and hey presto you will have found the feeding perch of a dragonfly.

On the Teifi, perhaps the most common of the dragonflies are the Common Red Darter and the Gold-ringed Dragonfly, but you may also see several other species including the fast-flying and very lovely Broad-bodied Chaser, with its blue and yellow body and iridescent wings.

A male Red Darter   **A Gold-ringed Dragonfly**

Understandably, upwinged flies get lots of attention from angling entomologists, and nearly all of the British species are present on the Teifi. While the Mayfly itself has only moderate hatches here, Iron Blues, Large Dark Olives and other members of the *Baëtis* family are rather more plentiful. Spring sometimes brings good hatches of March Browns, with Olive Uprights – a prolific fly throughout west Wales - even more abundant. In summer, the Blue-winged Olive is probably the most important upwinged fly, with the Pale Watery a close second.

Mayfly dun (female)   **Mayfly spinner (male)**

The Yellow May dun emerges from late spring right through to autumn (I have even seen them in October) and on warm summer evenings provides an opportunity for excellent dry fly fishing during the evening rise. The nymphs of this fly are flattened 'stone clingers', as also are the nymphs of the March Brown and the much more abundant Autumn Dun.

Stone-clinger nymphs are flattened like Formula 1 racing cars; they also have powerful legs to help them hold station in strong currents

Although the female spinners of upwinged flies are of most interest to flyfishers, it is the swarms of male spinners that we see far more often. Many of them, such as the Iron Blue, Pale Watery and Blue-winged Olive, have such brightly coloured bodies and crystal clear wings that it is a real treat to watch their dancing displays on bright summer evenings.

Iron Blue spinner (male)   **Blue-winged Olive spinner (male)**

Sedge flies are bigger than most other aquatic insects. The Grannom hatch of April is one of the first opportunities for dry fly fishers to practise their art, and the Teifi has tremendous hatches of this little buff sedge. In high summer the sedge hatch is mainly confined to late evenings, and Caperer and Large Cinnamon sedges are plentiful on the slower, reed-fringed stretches of the middle Teifi.

A Grannom sedge of springtime   **The Caperer, a sedge of summer**

Stoneflies are mainly spring and autumn insects. Early in the year the February Red emerges on the Teifi, while in autumn tiny Willow Flies and Needle Flies hatch all through the afternoons. One summer species, the Small Yellow Sally, can be seen on the river throughout the day in June and July.

Only the females of this Large Stonefly species have large wings; the males have very short wings and are unable to fly

Fish

Well, that is why anglers go fishing, isn't it? And naturally the Teifi has plenty to offer, both in terms of quantity, quality and variety of fish species. Sea Trout fishing in particular is a great attraction, and on the Teifi nowadays there are very good Sea Trout stocks. In the past they were largely confined to the lower reaches of the river, but now you can catch summer Sewin right up as far as Tregaron.

A 12 lb sewin from the Teifi

In a typical year between 2000 and 3000 Sea Trout are caught by Teifi anglers. Occasionally, as in 1996, the recorded rod catch rises to nearer 5000. Many anglers now recognise that the future of their sport is mainly in their own hands, and the number of Sewin being caught and released has risen greatly. About 40 per cent were returned in 1997, and by 2002 the figure had risen to 60 per cent.

An 11 lb autumn Salmon

Salmon fishing was once mainly a spring activity on the Teifi, but in recent years the runs have altered considerably. We still get spring salmon, but they are much less plentiful and the very large fish of thirty pounds and more have all but disappeared.

A wild Brown Trout holding station in a gentle current

The Brown Trout of the River Teifi have long been an attraction to visiting and local anglers. Numbers have declined in the past twenty years, but there are still some very fine wild brownies in parts of the river. Few anglers now take wild trout for the table, preferring to release them to add to the spawning stock.

The Grayling. Are these beautiful fish still present in the Teifi?

For many years there have been small numbers of Grayling between Lampeter and Llanybydder, although none have been reported as being caught on Llandysul A A waters since the mid 1990s.

The unimaginably weird head of a sea lamprey

Another migratory fish that enters the lower Teifi to spawn is the Sea Lamprey, an eel-like fish but one that migrates in the opposite direction to that of the eel, which spawns at sea. Lampreys are protected species, and if caught they must be returned to the river.

Although it is not widely known, there are in fact many other fish species in the Teifi including Sticklebacks, Stoneloaches, Eels and, of course, Minnows – the latter being by far the most abundant freshwater fish species in the British Isles.

Minnow   **Stoneloach**

The Bullhead, or Miller's Thumb, is protected under UK and European wildlife legislation. Bullheads are common on the River Teifi but quite scarce across Europe as a whole. These furtive little fish live in stony stretches of the river.

Many sea species, including Flounders, Dabs and Mullet, travel quite a long way into the freshwater reaches of the river, while from the rocky shores Mackerel, Pollack, Wrasse and the occasional Tope feature among the sea angler's catch.

Wrasse feed in rocky inlets all along the coast of West Wales

The Teifi Estuary is an important Bass nursery area. Bass grow extremely slowly, and so all small Bass that are caught must be returned to the water as quickly as possible. Bass can be caught from the rocky shores, from the beaches – especially after a storm – and by fishing offshore from dinghies or from charter boats.

Flyfishing for Bass has become a popular summer sport in Wales; the rocky shores around the Teifi Estuary can be particularly productive

Amphibians

As you wander along the banks of the Teifi in springtime, frogs and toads are to be seen everywhere. Frogs spawn early in the year – often before the last of the heavy frosts, and so a high proportion of potential offspring are lost.

In spring, Common Toads migrate as darkness descends, crossing roads to get to ponds and rivers where they lay their ribbons of spawn

Newts also migrate in the spring, and many are killed on the lanes beside the River Teifi as they leave marshland and swampy meadows and set off in search of deeper water in which to spawn.

One of a dozen Common Newts found on a lane one spring evening

Birds

Swan and signet on the lower Teifi

The wonderfully varied environment of the Teifi Valley, from wild mountains and moorland, to rich meadows and woodland, provides ideal habitats for a great variety of bird life. Tits, warblers and a host of other songbirds abound, and the Raven's sonorous croak punctuates most fishing days. Kingfishers, Herons, Grey Wagtails and Dippers are, of course, closely identified with rivers, and the Teifi is home to all of these. Dippers are particularly adept at collecting nymphs and larvae from the bed of shallow stretches of the river and from stony feeder streams, and their presence is an indication that the water quality is good.

A Dipper collecting caddis grubs   **The oh-so-patient Grey Heron**

From bank-side nests, Kingfishers dash up and down the river in search of food for their young. These beautiful birds are most abundant in lowland reaches of the Teifi and its tributaries, and there are Kingfishers throughout the Llandysul A A fisheries.

Catch of the day: the Kingfisher stuns its prey by banging it against the branch that it perches upon above the water, turning each little fish to swallow it head first

Grey Wagtails - often misidentified as Yellow Wagtails – can be seen perched precariously on stones in the shallow margins. Like the Dippers, they, too, are dependent upon insects for food.

A Grey Wagtail with three young chicks

A Flyfisher's Guide to the Teifi Valley

Peregrine Falcons, Buzzards, Owls and many other birds of prey live in West Wales. (Rumour has it that there is a Buzzard for each telegraph pole.) Of special significance is the Red Kite. Not so long ago the British population had fallen to single figures. Fortunately, from their last stronghold in the hills around Tregaron, Red Kites have made quite a comeback; we now have several hundreds and they are a frequent sight from the source of the Teifi to its estuary.

With their distinctive tails, Red Kites are easy to identify

Only rarely are Peregrine Falcons to be seen at such close range

Some birds are much less shy than others. Apart from when they are with young chicks, Mallard ducks will let you come quite close before they show any concern.

A Mallard drake sporting its brilliant headdress

A young Robin, its breast feathers not yet coloured up

That cheeky little Robin that hops along the hedgerow as if to escort you down to the river is often there to join you again on your return journey. The Robin's song is guaranteed to gladden the heart on even the most unpropitious of fishing days.

Seabirds soar over the West Wales cliff tops, their aerial displays are a great tourist attraction. A boat trip around the islands of the Pembrokeshire Coast, south of the Teifi Estuary, is a real treat for 'twitchers'. Puffins are the circus clowns; gannets the daredevil diving acrobats.

Gannets gather in dense colonies on the island of Grassholm, off the Pembrokeshire Coast

Mammals

Otters forage mainly along the margins of the river

The return of Otters to our rivers is generally seen as a sign that fish stocks are also improving. Some also say that the increase in Otter sightings has coincided with a noticeable reduction in the numbers of Mink; however, Water Voles are now rare, and the disastrous decline in their populations is being blamed mainly on Mink.

On the Teifi it is now a rare treat to catch a glimpse of 'Ratty', as Kenneth Grahame called the Water Vole in *Wind in the Willows*

You are, of course, likely to see many other mammals in the Teifi Valley. Waterside meadows that are (as they should be) spared from the plough and excessive pesticides and fertilisers, are home to rabbits, hares, mice and voles and – most 'unnoticeable' until you stumble over one on your way from a late-night sea trout fishing session – moles. What happens to Moley when the Teifi bursts its banks and floods the surrounding meadows? Moles are actually quite good swimmers, and so the chances are that Moley will be able to move into temporary accommodation on higher ground.

Moles can swim in freshwater, but perhaps they don't like salt: there are no moles on the other side of the Irish Sea!

But if you need one more reason to visit the Tefi it has to be for the diversity of sea mammals around the estuary and nearby coastal waters. Whales, dolphins, porpoises and seals provide great spectacles, and young seals are a particular attraction.

A seal pup on the island of Skomer, one of several wildlife sanctuaries off the beautiful Pembrokeshire Coast that are well worth a visit.

CHAPTER 6
Llandysul AA Constitution, Byelaws and Policies

By their very nature formal constitutions are unexciting documents; for a major angling club, however, a legal constitution is a necessity nowadays. Here, however, it might be of interest to readers of this book to know a little of how Llandysul A A is organised, how its policies are developed and who does what in the running of the club's affairs.

Aims and objectives

In the early days of a club, the constitution is rarely spelt out in a very precise way. In this respect Llandysul A A was quite typical. However, in 1965, when the club became a Company Limited by Guarantee, a formal Memorandum of Association was published. It says that Llandysul Angling Association was established to *'maintain, conduct and carry on an angling club for the convenience of the members of the Association... and to promote interest in the art of angling with rod and line, the proper conduct and etiquette of its members, and to instil interest in its members and the public generally in the maintenance and safeguarding of the streams and rivers in this country from pollution and other nuisance.'*

The Articles of Association described how the club was to be run: the maximum number of members (500); the need for an annual general meeting (currently held on the first Friday in December each year); the structure of the Council of Management - President, Chairman, Vice-chairman, Treasurer, Secretary and seven other members; the powers of the Council; the annual accounts and auditing; and disciplinary procedures.

In 1990 the club commissioned solicitors to update its constitution to reflect changes in company law since the formation of the club. The aims, objectives and structure of the club were not altered but a holding company, Llandysul Angling Association Limited, was established to manage the financial interests and to make all its fisheries assets available to the association. Control of Llandysul A A Ltd cannot be taken from the Teifi Valley, and should there come a time when for any reason the association has to be wound up, all assets will be made over to the Save the Children Fund.

Committee structure

The Limited Company structure comprises President, Chairman, Vice-chairman, Treasurer, Secretary and five ordinary members - ten in all. It would, of course, be possible for the AGM to vote for a complete change of club committee; if that were to happen, however, the limited company would maintain some essential continuity.

A turnover of membership is good for any management team, and so each year one third of Committee members stand down and the AGM elects new committee members. It is permissible for a member who stands down to be put up for re-election, and often that is the will of the AGM

Cyril Thomas (right) receiving an award in 1965

In 1965, the committee members were Thomas James Jones (President), William David Vivian Roderick (Chairman), Cyril Edward Montagu Hodding (Vice-chairman), Artie Jones (Hon Secretary), Timothy Davies (Treasurer), William Lloyd James, John Jones, David Emlyn Lewis, Cyril Thomas, David Rowland Timothy, Willie David Rees Williams.

In 1999 Llandysul A A celebrated its fiftieth anniversary. Of the committee of 1965, listed above, only Artie Jones continued to serve as an officer of the club in its fiftieth year. Artie stood down from the arduous role of Hon Sec in 2001, but until he died, in 2002, he continued to provide advice and help when asked – as indeed he was many times – by the new Hon Sec Tonlas Evans and by myself. The Association has commissioned a memorial plaque and stone, to be installed beside the River Teifi at Tyrdref, in recognition of the great service that Artie provided to Llandysul A A and to the wider local community.

Artie Jones, Llandysul A A's Hon Sec from 1965 to 2001

Llandysul A A Committee, 2004

As this book goes to print, Llandysul A A is served by the following committee of sixteen members, of whom ten (marked *) are the executive committee of Llandysul A A Ltd. They are listed here with some of the other duties they carry out:

Member	Office	Other responsibilities
Dr David Roberts*	President	Conservation sub-committee; policy development
Dr Ian Thomas*	Chairman	Catch return records; newsletters; website; policy development
Tonlas Evans*	Secretary	General management; events; policy development
John Jones*	Treasurer	Accounts and VAT; policy development
Alan Williams*	Vice- chairman	Permits; policy; riverbank maintenance
Gwilym Jones*	Vice- president	Membership records; permits; events; conservation; newsletter distribution
Melvin Grey	Member	Conservation; minutes; events; policy
Ieuan Thomas*	Member	Conservation work; events; policy
Eirig Thomas*	Member	Conservation work; events; policy development
David Williams*	Member	Riverbank maintenance; events; policy
Dewi Roberts	Member	Competitions; policy; events
Wyn Evans	Member	Riverbank maintenance; events; policy
Raymond Jones	Member	Events; policy
Eric Davies	Member	Events; policy
(Place vacant)	Member	
Pat O'Reilly*	Life Member	Newsletters; website

Tonlas Evans, Llandysul A A's Hon Sec since 2001, has done a great deal to improve our relationships with landowners and with other organisations that have an interest in the River Teifi. The day-to-day management of a club such as ours makes substantial demands upon the Secretary's time.

How the committee operates

Committee now meets on an as-required basis, making extensive use of email communication between meetings. When there is a major development - for example proposals for changes to the rod fishing byelaws or net limitation orders - additional meetings are often necessary. Then the committee discusses the content of its intended responses to the Environment Agency, Countryside Council for Wales or Welsh Assembly Government, prior to them being drafted by the chairman and secretary.

Dr David Roberts, Llandysul Angling Association president since 1986

Meetings of the committees of Llandysul A A Ltd and the angling association are held on the same evening. Members of the limited company generally meet for no more than five minutes immediately after the main meeting; their primary tasks is to ratify financial recommendations of sub-committees and working groups.

Club committee meetings can last for three hours if there is a weighty agenda, and occasionally it has been necessary to adjourn and reconvene later in the week to complete work on particularly complex issues. (The Salmon and Freshwater Fisheries Review and proposals for byelaw changes are typical examples.)

Sub-committees deal with specialist topic areas and report back to the club committee on their work and any matters arising. The number of sub-committees varies from time to time, but in recent years the Conservation and Riverbank Maintenance teams have been active almost continually.

Rogues' Gallery

Committee member David Williams, son of our first Hon Sec

Committee member Alan Williams (permit sales, Lampeter)

Dewi Roberts is Llandysul A A's Competitions Secretary

Eirig Thomas, long-term committee member and Dewi's predecessor

Long-serving committee member Ieuan Thomas

John Jones, our Treasurer, happy with the state of the accounts

Llandysul A A Byelaws

1. Status of byelaws

These byelaws are made, and may from time to time be repealed, by the Executive Committee pursuant to the rules of the Association. They are binding on all members of the Association as if they were part of the rules themselves.

2. Conduct

a) Members shall at all times conduct themselves in such a way as to uphold the good name and reputation of the Association.

b) Members shall not, either individually or acting in conjunction with others, make any statement or enter into any agreement likely to place the Association's acquisition, tenure, protection or development of fisheries in jeopardy.

c) Any disputes shall be settled by the Executive Committee whose decision shall be final.

3. Election of members

a) Unless otherwise decided by the Executive Committee, either generally or in any particular case, applications for membership of the Association shall be made in writing in such form and containing such details as the Executive Committee shall from time to time require and shall be accompanied by one copy of a passport photograph of the applicant.

b) Every application for membership shall be considered by the Chairman and Secretary (or by such other members of the Executive Committee as they may at any time appoint for the purpose) who may, at their discretion, either accept the application or reject it without having to state any reason, or refer it to the Executive Committee for a decision.

c) Upon election or admission to membership, and after payment of any applicable entrance fee and subscription, the members shall be issued with a membership ticket together with an identity card bearing his or her passport photograph.

4. Membership

a) Members must be in possession of valid membership tickets and authorised identity cards at all times when fishing on Association waters.

b) Any person found fishing on Association waters and not possessing a valid membership ticket is liable to prosecution.

c) Any members, finding another person fishing on Association waters, should challenge that person and, upon producing their own membership ticket, demand to see proof of that person's membership. Upon failure to reply with this request, the name and address of the trespasser and their vehicle registration number should, if possible, be noted and reported without delay to the Secretary.

5. Access to waters

a) Membership entitles members to walk only over ground adjoining Association fishing waters. Access to Association waters must only be gained via the approved access routes shown on the Association's maps, and members must close all gates where provided.

b) Members must not wilfully damage, and must at all times seek to avoid damaging, crops, fences and other property.

c) Members must not take dogs onto Association waters.

d) The Association's car parking facilities are not to be used for sleeping purposes.

e) Motor vehicles are prohibited from entering the private road to Rhydygalfe Farm.

f) Parking is prohibited on the farmyard or on the lane leading to the farm on the Maesisaf waters (beat 7).

6. Conservation

a) Bag limits throughout the Association's waters are as follows:
- A rod limit of four trout per day
- A rod limit of four sewin (sea trout) per day. To protect whitling stocks all sewin less than 12 inches in length (measured from the nose to the cleft in the tail) must be carefully returned to the river.
- A limit of two salmon per day or five salmon per week
- Having caught any one of the above bag limits, a member must immediately cease fishing.

b) Between 1st June and 31st August, spinning is prohibited between the hours of sunset and sunrise.

c) Worm fishing is prohibited between the hours of sunset and sunrise.

d) The sale of rod-caught fish from Association waters is prohibited.

Carefully releasing wild trout and salmon helps to conserve stocks

7. Fishing regulations

a) No member shall stand closer than fifteen yards from the next fisherman when fishing on Association waters.

b) A limit of one hour is allowed to a member in the event of another member waiting to fish the same pool for salmon; and no angler shall remain in one position on the riverbank for more than an hour when other members are waiting to fish. When night fishing for sewin the one hour limit includes waiting time.

c) Members having odd-numbered tickets are entitled to fish particular beats from 12 noon on odd-numbered days to 12 noon on the following day. Even numbered tickets allow fishing from 12 noon on even days until 12 noon the following day. This byelaw applies to:

- Jacks Pool on Brynhawc Waters (beat 8)
- All of Cwmmackwith fishery (beat 10)
- All of the Rhydygalfe fishery(beat 13)
- Black Pool on the Tan-y-Coed fishing (beat 13a)

d) Certain stretches are designated 'flyfishing only'. These are:

- The whole of the Cellan fishery (beat 2)
- The whole of Llettytwppa (beat 3) on and between 1st June and 31st August
- Brynhawc waters (beat 8) from the tail of Prysg Pool to Vicars Run, but excluding Vicars Pool itself

e) Schoolchildren holding Trout Fishing tickets are limited to a line not exceeding 4lb breaking strain, hooks no larger than size eight and, if bait fishing, not more than one worm on the hook. When spinning, they may not use minnows or other artificial baits larger than $1^{1}/_{2}$ inches in length.

f) Float fishing is prohibited throughout Association waters.

Members are also required to observe all statutory national and local byelaws, including close season dates and method restrictions, as published by the Environment Agency and approved by the Welsh Assembly Government.

Schoolchildren may fish for trout on our waters for just £2 per year; they must use tackle appropriate to the size of fish they are seeking to catch.

Conservation Policy of Llandysul A A

In our club rules, and any emergency measures we may impose upon ourselves, we will apply the precautionary principle to our migratory fish stocks. In the absence of expert scientific advice, we will give priority to spawning escapement rather than risking over-exploitation, even though other factors (such as high-seas netting) outside our control have major impacts on run size.

Sustainable exploitation

By means of bag limits, time and method restrictions, and other restrictions where appropriate, we will endeavour to limit exploitation of fish in our waters so that the stocks are self-sustaining without artificial enhancement stocking.

Hatchery stocking

We will endeavour to use our hatchery facility as an insurance against pollution damage on the Teifi. We will also use it to prime the recovery of spawning and nursery tributaries by seeding juvenile fish in areas restored by habitat improvement work or opened up by the removal of obstructions to the passage of fish.

Regulation

We will campaign for firm but fair statutory regulations to be strictly enforced on both rod and net fisheries to conserve fish stocks, and in particular any endangered species or components of migratory fish runs on our river (for example multi-sea-winter spring Salmon).

Predation

We accept that predation by birds and animals is a natural and essential feature of a healthy fishery. We will not support a policy of management by widespread culling of wild creatures unless, in the opinion of recognised experts, other control measures including habitat management have been fully explored and utilised.

Riverbank management

We will endeavour to retain a natural riverside environment. We will therefore carry out the minimum of tree trimming and bank clearance consistent with safe access for fishing and passage along the riverbank. We will not remove native plants or trees merely to make fishing easy.

Education

We will endeavour to influence other river users, the public, magistrates, councillors, MPs and Government to adopt policies and behaviour that protect river fisheries, their stocks and habitat. We will encourage young people to take an interest in the countryside and in the river environment and its conservation.

CHAPTER 7
Membership Services and Fact Sheets

When considering joining an angling club, good fishing is naturally a high priority, but members also need accurate maps and access information and well-maintained stiles, paths and footbridges. In addition, for many of us a little guidance on what to expect - the terrain, the nature of the river banks and wading conditions for example - can make all the difference between a pleasant day out and a thoroughly frustrating and possibly hazardous experience.

This chapter contains a selection of the information available to members via:

- Newsletters at least twice per year
- An interactive CD-ROM guide to the Teifi Valley and its fishing
- A programme of Welcome Day events
- Free flyfishing lessons for children
- A website with beat maps, the latest news, catch statistics, tackle shops etc
- Fact Sheets on angling safety, Teifi fly life, and catch statistics

Current Affairs
Newsletter of Llandysul Angling Association
November 2004

In this issue:
> Letter from the Secretary   2
> AGM Arrangements and Subscription Proposals   3
> Celtic Rivers Trust Partnership   4
> Sea Trout Success   6
> Salmon Award - How to Enter   7
> Wildlife Corner - Disappearing Beauties   8
> Spring Welcome Day 2004 - Report   9
> Competition News - Pysgotwr Plu Llandysul   10
> Young Conservationists and Flyfishing Lessons - Report   11
> Catch results for 2003   13
> Renewing your Membership for 2005   14
> Books for Christmas   15
> Farewell Message from the Outgoing Chairman   16

Written and designed by Paul O'Reilly, Gelyn Elpals, Tre-bach Estraine, Llandysul SA44 5HD
© 2004, Llandysul Angling Association. All Rights Reserved.

Current Affairs, Llandysul A A's twice yearly newsletter, keeps members up to date with the club's developments and events. Special editions are produced whenever we have news for members that will not keep until the next scheduled edition.

A Flyfisher's Guide to the Teifi Valley

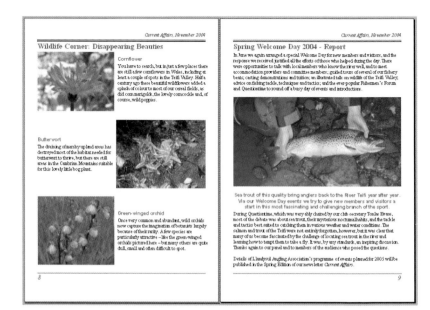

Two pages from the Spring 2004 edition of *Current Affairs*

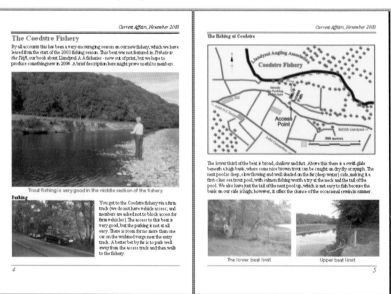

Coedstre Fishery details, in *Current Affairs* November 2003

Multimedia Guide to Fishing in the Teifi Valley

Our Multimedia Guide to Fishing in the Teifi Valley was published in 2004, with financial assistance from the Welsh Assembly Government's *Adfywio Cefn Gwlad – Rural Recovery* Programme. The design and development took nearly a year, and I am grateful to those members who have allowed their pictures to be included in this interactive CD-ROM.

Aware that many problems are caused by malicious computer programs that contain viruses and 'Trojan Horse' scripts capable of damaging computers and destroying valuable data, we have ensured that our CD-ROM runs without installing any program files on the user's PC. To achieve this it was necessary to write scripts that make use of modules of software already existing on most computers, and so the 'browser' that you see when the Teifi Valley CD-ROM is in use is actually an overlay running on top in Microsoft's Internet Explorer web browser. (When you close down our CD you will see that Internet Explorer continues running until you close it down too.) In practice, our CD runs with all features on about 98 per cent of PCs; it functions reasonably well on PCs running non-Microsoft browsers, and it can be browsed like a website on Macintosh computers. This, we think, is a good compromise between security and functionality.

Our CD-ROM gives full details of not only river and stillwater game fisheries in the Teifi Valley but also of a range of coarse and sea angling opportunities available in the local area.

So what does it actually do?

As well as details about fishing, there are interactive puzzles, details of wildlife, ecology and scenic beauty in and around the Teifi Valley; information about where to stay and good places to eat out; and, of course, Llandysul A A beat guides plus road, rail and air travel information to help visitors to the valley.

Our CD is not just pictures and text: video clips are also included.

Wildflowers and fungi of the Teifi Valley are an added attraction to many of our visitors, as they are to those who live here. The CD contains a few examples of the many beautiful species to be found here.

Each of Llandysul A A's fisheries is featured, with pictures, maps and fishing advice. There are also aerial photographs and rotating panoramas of several of the fishing beats.

Our Website

Llandysul A A was one of the first angling clubs to recognise the potential of the Internet. In 1996 we began building our website www.fishing-in-wales.com and within two years it contained details and maps of each of our fishing beats as well as summary information about most other game, coarse and sea fishing venues in Wales. We have provided this information service to help\our own members and visitors to Wales, because there has been no national investment by Wales Tourist Board to provide such a facility.

Thankfully, the situation is now improved, and professionals are being funded by the Welsh Assembly Government to publicise the fisheries of Wales on www.fishing.visitwales.com - the new Wales Tourist Board website. From spring 2004, therefore, the Fishing in Wales website will focus on the needs of visitors to the Teifi Valley.

The home page of our website, November 2004

The visitor rate to our website has risen steadily since its launch more than eight years ago, and by the autumn of 2002 we were already receiving two million separate site visits per year. Members of Llandysul A A, many of whom live a long way from the Teifi Valley, say that they make regular use of the website not only for the fishing information it contains but also for the two thousand or so other pages of fisheries, wildlife and ecology pictures and information that we have published there over the years.

A Flyfisher's Guide to the Teifi Valley

Llandysul A A's commitment to helping young people has been greatly facilitated by the availability of the Internet. Not only do we have a section of our website reserved for young members and visitors to our club waters, but we have also published quizzes and interactive puzzles there. The Web has also been our main vehicle for publicising the free flyfishing lessons and conservation activities that we have arranged for local and visiting young people.

Via our Young Members pages we publicise opportunities for schoolchildren, parents and teachers to take part in river surveys and other conservation activities.

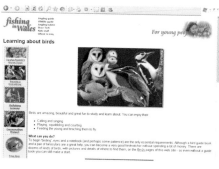

Young birdwatchers can find information on a good selection of species to be seen in gardens, in open country and at the waterside.

There is, of course, quite a lot of fishing information for youngsters, including details of the free tuition provided by Llandysul A A during the school holidays.

Welcome Days

Our series of Welcome Days has been particularly popular with newcomers to Llandysul A A fisheries on the Teifi. These are opportunities to meet local anglers who know the river well; to see some of the beats and have a free casting lesson; to attend illustrated talks about the wildlife and fishing on our river and join in the question-and-answer sessions afterwards; and to meet and talk with accommodation providers and committee members, all of whom are keen to help make your visits to the Teifi more enjoyable.

David Williams, whose enthusiastic and authoritative contributions to Welcome Day events are particularly appreciated by newcomers to our Teifi fisheries.

Whenever possible through the season, we put on impromptu events of this kind for groups of visitors. Near the start of they season, however, it is particularly nice to be able to meet, welcome and offer help to new members and others who have not yet found their way around all of our thirty miles or so of fishing on the Teifi.

Casting demonstrations and free casting instruction are a great help those who are new to river fishing

Typical timetable for Welcome Day events

11-30am	Meet at The Porth Hotel, Llandysul. (Coffee and biscuits.) Illustrated talk about the wildlife and fisheries of the Teifi Valley. Questions and answers plus our annual wildlife and fishing quiz.
12-30pm	Meet accommodation providers, committee and local members
1-00pm	Lunch (for those who so wish) at The Porth Hotel
2-00pm	Casting demonstrations and introductory tuition by qualified flyfishing instructors at our Tyrdref fishing beat in Llandysul (just a 250-yard walk from The Porth Hotel).
3-00pm	Guided visits to several of the Llandysul A A fisheries, with opportunities to discuss tackle, techniques and tactics with successful local anglers.
6-30pm	Dinner (for those who so wish) at The Porth Hotel
7-45pm	Illustrated talk on fishing the Teifi for salmon, trout and sea trout, followed by a question and answer session
8-45pm	Fishers' Forum: put your questions to a panel of local experts
9-30pm on	Sea trout fishing on the Teifi (for members and permit holders)

Casting tuition is included in the Welcome Day programme

An illustrated talk is part of the Welcome Day introduction

Hon Sec Tonlas Evans chairing Fisher's Forum in 2003

Who can take part and what does it cost?

All are welcome to take part in the Welcome Day events. Except for the fishing session in the evening, it is not necessary to be a member or even to hold a visitor permit - and apart from accommodation and meals, everything is free of charge.

Local accommodation providers are invited to join us at The Porth Hotel from 11-30am, when they have an opportunity to welcome our guests and help us make them feel welcome. Maps, CD-ROMs and other Llandysul A A publicity materials are also distributed during the Welcome Day programme.

Flyfishing Lessons for Young People

Junior membership of Llandysul A A , trout fishing only, costs just £2 per year (with no joining fee), as it has for the past twenty years and more. Not surprisingly we get a lot of young people - locals and visitors - interested in joining our club. To help them get started safely with every prospect of early success we provide free lessons during the school summer holidays. The tuition, provided by qualified professional instructors covers:

- Safety, angling etiquette, tackle selection, assembly and maintenance
- Casting techniques - basics and the more advanced casts
- River life - fish, insects and water birds
- Flyfishing techniques and basic tactics

Volunteers help to set up tackle for flyfishing lessons, summer 2004

Casting competition

Each year the girls and boys who take part in our programme of flyfishing tuition, have the opportunity to enter a casting accuracy competition, with a prize of fishing tackle for the winner. There is also a special award for good sportsmanship. Since Derek Hoskin and I began giving the lessons, in 1987, over a thousand young people have taken part; several are now extremely competent flyfishers and two have fished in the Welsh Junior team. Special thanks are due to Derek, who helped youngsters in this way for fifteen years. Sue Parker has also helped in recent years, and I am delighted that Eric Davies and Peter Jones – both long-term members of Llandysul A A - are now qualified and committed to continuing the youth tuitoion programme.

The aim is to enable young anglers to enjoy fishing success in safety.

Learning to locate the lies that trout take up in a river.

The casting competition, with an emphasis on accuracy rather than distance, is always lots of fun.

Conservation Projects for Young People

Since 1987 we have involved young people in practical work to monitor and protect wildlife via a programme of activities that we call the Young Conservationists initiative. The aim is to help young people to learn about water life and the animals and birds that live beside streams, and to encourage them to protect and care for the environment. Publicity, both in the newspapers and on radio and television programmes starring our Young Conservationists, has also helped to raise public awareness of environment issues and to encourage participation in other initiatives to help restore and protect damaged and degraded wildlife habitats.

While setting up and running these events, we have been able to develop a useful set of learning resources; these, in the form of a CD-ROM, we have been able to make freely available to other angling clubs and wildlife groups in the UK as well a number of conservation bodies overseas.

Fish stock survey on the River Cerdin

In a project on the River Cerdin, we fenced off a buffer strip to prevent cattle grazing right to the water's edge, created gaps in trash dams to allow fish to migrate in low flows, and 'skylighted' closed in areas to encourage weed growth. With help from staff of Environment Agency Wales, our Young Conservationists surveyed fish, insect and plant life before the habitat improvement work and for several years afterwards. There was a substantial increase in juvenile salmon and trout numbers as a result of the work carried out to improve this important Teifi feeder stream.

Keeping proper records

Young Conservationists are encouraged keep records of the results of the findings of their surveys. We have published their results each year in a set of Young Conservationists Project pages on our website. Here are two sample screen shots:

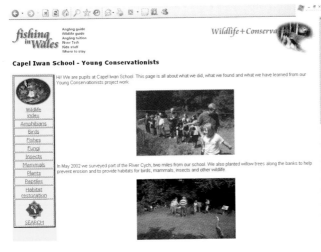

Each school is offered its own web page, illustrating the activities and results of the work undertaken by pupils from the school.

Although they have help with creating and uploading their web pages, it is the children themselves who decide what information goes onto their pages.

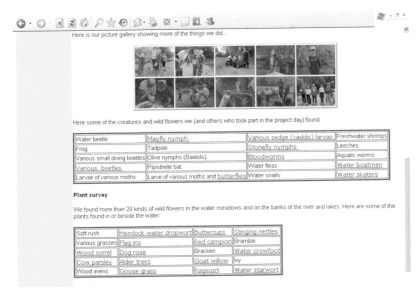

Here is our picture gallery showing more of the things we did...

Here some of the creatures and wild flowers we (and others who took part in the project day) found:

Water beetle	Mayfly nymph.	Various sedge (caddis) larvae	Freshwater shrimps
Frog	Tadpole	Stonefly nymphs	Leeches
Various small diving beetles	Olive nymphs (Baetids)	Bloodworms	Aquatic worms
Various beetles	Pipistrelle bat	Water fleas	Water boatmen
Larvae of various moths	Larve of various moths and butterflies	Water snails	Water skaters

Plant survey

We found more than 20 kinds of wild flowers in the water meadows and on the banks of the river and lakes. Here are some of the plants found in or beside the water:

Soft rush	Hemlock water dropwort	Buttercups	Stinging nettles
Various grasses	Flag iris	Red campion	Bramble
Wood sorrel	Dog rose	Bracken	Water crowfoot
Cow parsley	Alder trees	Goat willow	Ivy
Wood avens	Goose grass	Ragwort	Water starwort

Safety Guidance

Unless you take a few basic precautions, fishing is potentially a very dangerous pursuit, and each year several anglers are injured or die in tragic accidents most of which could have been avoided. These basic guidelines will help you to minimise the risks to yourself, to others and to the wildlife of rivers and lakes. Please note that in some places there may be other hazards not listed here, and so always check with the fishery owner or manager and observe the fishery rules.

Eye protection, a torch, a life preserver and a wading staff are important safety equipment on the Teifi.

Buoyancy aids should always be worn on top of other clothing such as a fishing vest or a raincoat.

Personal safety on rivers

Every year many strong swimmers lose their lives in rivers. The force and the turbulent nature of the current can make it difficult to scramble out, especially where banks are high. Areas where the river flows over bedrock or through narrow gorges should be approached with great caution and wearing a buoyancy aid and suitable (felted or studded) footwear.

If you should fall in, use your arms to protect your head. Roll onto your back and kick with your legs until you reach shallower water. Chest or thigh waders will not pull you under (as is sometimes suggested); indeed, they tend to trap air and add to your natural buoyancy. However, they can increase the weight you have to drag up the bank.

Beware of undercut banks. Especially after rain they can fall in on you as you wade beneath them. More often a collapse occurs as you approach the edge of a high bank, when both you and the bank could fall in, perhaps onto another angler. Deep undercuts are especially likely on the outside of bends in the watercourse. Keep well back from the edge when passing these hazards.

If you can't swim then be wary of wading - even in the shallower stretches of the river. If you must wade then a wading staff can improve your stability. Look out for submerged tree roots or boulders, which often have depressions upstream and alongside. (Lamprey redds cut in spring can be hard to spot once the gravel is coated in algae.) Rivers can rise in level rapidly and catch you unawares. It may be fine where you are fishing, but it could be raining heavily in the hills and your path to safety may quickly be cut off.

Wading in coloured water where you cannot see the bottom is very risky. A spate can cause gravel to shift so that what was once a safe area becomes a death trap. For the same reason, wade a pool at night only if you have surveyed it by day – and don't assume that last year's 'recce' is still valid: rivers change!

Should you discover another angler in difficulty out of his or her depth, first look for something to bridge the gap between you - a piece of driftwood, a landing net handle, even your fishing rod - rather than jump in and risk a double tragedy. (Of course, courageous acts can be justified when there is no alternative, provided you are a strong swimmer and, ideally, have had life-saving training.)

Personal safety on lakes

Many natural upland lakes, including Teifi Pools, have areas where the bank is steep and rocky. When bank fishing, choose footwear that offers a secure grip. Leather soled shoes are particularly dangerous on rocks, as are rubber-soled waders without metal studs.

When fishing from a boat, wear a buoyancy aid and cast, retrieve line and net your fish without standing up. The reduction in noise and your reduced visibility will improve your chances of success. (You rarely need to cast far if you keep low!)

Wear goggles, spectacles or sunglasses for eye protection, and cast so that your line is well away from your boat partner or boatman. Encourage them to wear eye protection too.

On large waters, don't take risks: take suitable clothing with you. If the boat has an engine make sure that there is sufficient fuel onboard and that there are oars and a baler in case of emergency. If the weather threatens to turn squally, return to shore without delay.

Safe Use of Fishing Tackle

Carbon fishing rods conduct electricity, and so do not cast near overhead power lines. It is also wise to put away your fishing rod whenever there is lightning nearby.

Keep a safe distance from other river users when casting, and let other anglers know if you intend passing behind them. Some anglers are hard of hearing; so, having called out, make sure you get a reply before entering their casting zone.

Use scissors to cut nylon; don't attempt to break it with your hands, or you could easily end up with a very painful cut. And similarly, if your fly gets snagged and you cannot work it free, break away safely. One way is to wrap the line around a sleeve of your coat to obtain a safe grip before turning your back and tensioning the line until it breaks.

When using spey or snake roll casts, the direction of the wind determines which casting techniques can be used safely; choose the wrong cast and the fly could easily hit you in the face, which could be particularly serious if you are not wearing eye protection at the time.

Protection of Wildlife

Never discard nylon or other kinds of leader material at the waterside: it can injure and kill birds and other small creatures. Roll up used nylon and cut it into short lengths before taking it home to burn it. In this way, should you accidentally drop it, there is no risk to wildlife. Never leave flies hanging from trees, because birds or bats could seize them with disastrous consequences. To recover tackle caught in branches overhanging the water, use a pole rather than climbing the tree.

To avoid risks to birds and other wildlife, do not discard used flies or line by the riverside. Always take used tackle and litter home, where you can dispose of it responsibly.

Protect trees, bushes and marginal weed beds; they are home to numerous small creatures. Aquatic weed also harbours insect life essential to the health of the river. These insects in turn form a vital part of the food supply for young sea trout salmon.

Grazing animals can die if they ingest discarded nylon or plastic litter

Fly Life of the Teifi Valley

During 1995 and 1996, Melvin Grey and I carried out a survey of the water life of the River Teifi as part of the research for a book, *Matching the Hatch*, which was subsequently published in 1997.

A Mayfly Dun: the Teifi now has sparse hatches of *Ephemera danica*

We found several species not generally thought to occur this far westward. We also discovered that at that time the fly life of the Teifi was much more diverse than that of the rich chalk streams of southern England. Members who fish for trout may find useful this summary of our findings.

Alder flies are a common sight on the River Teifi in springtime

Upwinged flies - *Ephemeroptera*

Common name	Genera and species	Peak time	Abundance
Mayfly	*Ephemera danica*	Spring	moderate
Olive upright	*Rithrogena semicolorata*	Spring	high
March brown	*Rithrogena germanica*	Spring	moderate
Autumn dun	*Ecdyonurus dispar*	Autumn	moderate
Large brook dun	*Ecdyonurus torrentis*	Spring	moderate
Large green dun	*Ecdyonurus insignis*	Summer	low
Yellow may	*Heptagenia sulphurea*	Spring	high
Dusky yellowstreak	*Heptagenia lateralis*	Summer	moderate
Purple dun	*Paraleptophlebia cincta*	Summer	low
Turkey brown	*Paraleptophlebia submarginata*	Spring	very low
Blue-winged olive	*Ephemerella ignita*	Summer	high
Large dark olive	*Baetis rhodani*	Spring	moderate
Medium olive	*Baetis vernus; Baetis tenax*	Summer	high
Small dark olive	*Baetis scambus*	Summer	high
Iron blue	*Baetis muticus*	Summer	high
Pale watery	*Baetis fuscatus*	Summer	high
Pale evening dun	*Procloeon bifidum*	Summer	moderate
Small spurwing	*Centroptilum luteolum*	Summer	high
Large spurwing	*Centroptilum pennulatum*	Summer	moderate
Caenis fly	*Caenis* and *Brachycercus* species	Summer	high

***Ecdyonurus torrentis* – the nymph of the Autumn Dun**

Two rather surprising omissions are the late March brown, *Ecdyonurus venosus*, which is common on many spate rivers, and the sepia dun, *Leptophlebia marginata*. The latter is found in some North Wales rivers, but it would be interesting to hear from anyone who has positively identified these species in the Teifi Valley.

Sedge flies - *Trichoptera*

Common name	Genera and species	Peak time	Abundance
Grannom	*Brachycentrus subnubilus*	Spring	high
Brown sedge	*Anabolia nervosa*	Autumn	moderate
Brown silverhorn sedge	*Athripsodes albifrons*	Summer	high
Caperer	*Halesus radiatus*	Autumn	moderate
Sand fly	*Rhyacophila dorsalis*	Summer	moderate
Cinnamon sedge	*Limnephilus lunatus*	Spring	moderate
Large cinnamon sedge	*Potamophylax latipennis*	Summer	high
Grouse wing	*Mystacides longicornis*	Summer	moderate
Welshman's button	*Sericostoma personatum*	Summer	high
Marbled sedge	*Hydropsyche instabilis*	Summer	low
Black sedge	*Silo nigricornis*	Summer	high
Yellow spotted sedge	*Philopotamus montanus*	Spring	moderate
Black silverhorn	*Mystacides nigra*	Summer	high

Sedge flies come in one shape and all sizes

Stoneflies - *Plecoptera*

Common name	Genera and species	Peak time	Abundance
February red	*Brachyptera risi*	Spring	low
Large stonefly	*Perlodes microcephala*	Spring	moderate
Small yellow sally	*Chloroperla torrentium*	Summer	high
Yellow sally	*Isoperla grammatica*	Summer	high
Needle fly	*Leuctra fusca*	Autumn	high
Small brown	*Nemoura cinerea*	Summer	low

True flies - *Diptera*

Common name	Genera and species	Peak time	Abundance
Black gnat	*Bibio johannis*	Spring	moderate
Hawthorn fly	*Bibio marci*	Spring	high
Medium craneflies	*Tipulidae*	Summer	high
Daddy-long-legs	*Tipula maxima*	Autumn	high
Reed smuts	*Simulium species*	Summer	moderate
Large green midge	*Chironomus plumosus*	Summer	high

Many other insects, including water bugs and beetles, contribute to the diet of fish in the Teifi. This nymph of the Great Diving Beetle will eat the eggs and alevins of trout and salmon if it gets the chance, but in turn it could also become a welcome meal for a trout or a salmon parr.

Catch Results

Since 1983, Dr Ian Thomas has maintained records of catches of salmon and sea trout on Llandysul A A waters. The statistics are published each year in the club newsletter, *Current Affairs.* Until 1998 only around 60 per cent of members submitted catch returns (although we believe that the majority of missing returns would have been nil catches). In 1998 the AGM agreed that submission of a annual catch return would become a mandatory prerequisite of continuing membership; since then all members' catches have been included in the published results.

Here are the Llandysul A A total catch figures for recent years:

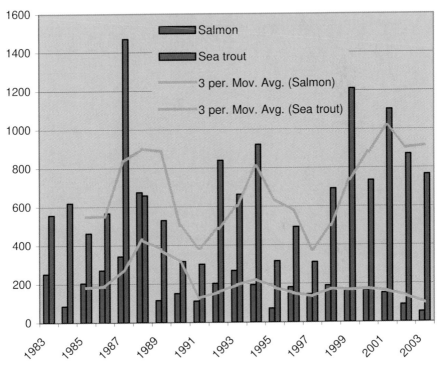

The total salmon and sewin catch for the Teifi mirrors our results reasonably well, with 1988 being a bumper year for salmon and 1987 being the best year in recent times for sea trout. Teifi sea trout stocks (based upon catches and counter data up to 2003) appear to be doing well. The three-year moving average trend line shows the characteristic cyclic nature with an overall steady level or a marginally upward shift over the past 20 years.

The news on salmon stocks is not so good, however, and the trend line shows a relentless decline overlaid by the usual cyclic pattern. This is despite the introduction in 1998 of byelaws to protect spring salmon.

The pattern of catches through the 2002 season is also interesting, as it shows that the majority of the salmon caught on the Teifi run in autumn, whereas sea trout provide good sport from May to October:

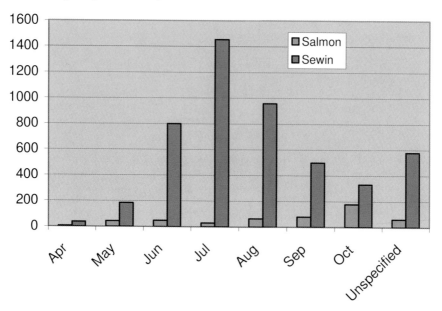

For the 2002 season, anglers reported catching 507 salmon and 4841 sea trout on the Teifi. Of these 234 salmon and 2076 sea trout were released to add to the spawning stock. Llandysul A A members have made an above average contribution to the efforts to conserve salmon stocks; our catch-and-release rate is above the Teifi average and we also have a ban on the sale of rod-caught fish as a deterrent to 'fishmongers' applying for membership. Anyone found selling salmon or sea trout is subject to an automatic expulsion from the club. Thankfully, we have never had cause to invoke this rule.

As this book goes to press, Government is consulting on what further measures, if any, should be taken to help restore salmon stocks across England and Wales. The committee of Llandysul A A actively supports efforts to restore and protect spawning and nursery habitats in the feeder streams. We also see the need for closer monitoring and enforcement of pollution control regulations – in particular the need for better control of sheep dipping processes and the removal from the market of synthetic pyrethroid dips that are lethally toxic to freshwater invertebrates.

A major cause of the continuing decline of our salmon stocks is the harvesting of salmon of unknown and mixed origins in the drift-net fishery off the western coast of Ireland. This mixed-stock exploitation may well exceed to legal rod catch on the Teifi and other Welsh rivers. We continue to lobby the Irish government, urging them to comply with international legislation and scientific advice.

CHAPTER 8
Llandysul A A - a brief history

In one sense at least, angling clubs must have been in existence since sport fishing began. They would have been informal affairs, of course, owning no waters and doing little more than organise the occasional fishing excursion for groups of friends. But when did the angling clubs that we know today come in to existence?

Ellem Angling Club, at Berwick, was founded in 1829 and claims to be the oldest angling club in the world. The Houghton Fishing-Club, established in 1822, may appear to predate its northern rival, but as far as I can ascertain it was some twenty years later before the Houghton Club actually secured fishing of its own.

By comparison, Llandysul A A is a relative youngster. Founded in the winter of 1948-49, after a shaky start the club grew rapidly and is now owns probably more top-quality fishing rights than any other Welsh angling association. The story of Llandysul A A's development is, I think, quite remarkable.

The Porth Hotel – focal point for Llandysul anglers for over 100 years

False starts

Had initial attempts to form an angling club on the middle Teifi been successful, Llandysul Angling Association would now be one of the oldest clubs in the world. In 1861, anglers in the village of Llandysul made their first recorded attempt at forming an Association, with the aim of protecting and generally improving fishing. At that time the Teifi Estuary was intensively fished by netsmen. There were sixteen draught nets; and a fixed net was used in the river itself down to the bridge at Cardigan. Above this there were other nets, known locally as jackass nets. On the six miles of river between Llechryd Bridge and Cenarth Bridge some 300 coracles operated; the coraclemen claimed the right to do so based on long and undisputed usage. And then there was perhaps the greatest of all obstacles the salmon had to face: a fish trap at Cenarth Weir.

In 1860, the close season for nets did not begin until 3rd November, and by all accounts even this restriction was observed only partially. At the time the River Teifi was also seriously threatened by pollution from four lead mines, which were working near its source. The salmon were under siege; something had to be done.

In 1867 a board of Conservators was formed. In the following year the conservators began to blow up the obstructive rocks at Cenarth Falls so that fish could ascend the falls and so make use of the abundance of spawning beds in the upper Teifi. The local inhabitants at Cenarth were not at all happy with this plan. They stoned the workmen, whose tools, barrows, and planks were broken up and thrown into the river. At that time just 23 salmon rod licences were issued for the Teifi, at a £1 each. In comparison, there were 23 seine nets at 31s 6d and some 91 coracles at 10s 6d each. Even by 1895 the number of licensed salmon rod fishermen has increased to 41 for the whole of the River Teifi.

It had long been the custom of draught-net fishermen in the public waters below Cardigan to take turns to join two of their nets together. The two nets joined to make a length of nearly 400 yards, which was stretched right across the estuary so that every salmon that fell back witb the tide was caught in the Shot Fawr. In this method of fishing each fisherman had a chance of becoming a Shot Fawr once in every five days. The rewards could be great: it is recorded that as many as 170 salmon had been taken at a single shot. In times of drought this net would capture the fish that had gathered together to await a flood.

Complaints were made to the Board of Conservators that the great killing power of this net was ruining the Teifi fisheries, and in 1895 the riparian owners, the anglers and the coracle fishermen proposed that a byelaw should be introduced to abolish the Shot Fawr, and it ceased to exist from 1896.

With the Shot Fawr removed from the estuary, you might have expected the angling associations to go from strength to strength, but this was not the case. The club at Llandysul was compelled to break up in 1897 due to lack of funds. In 1924, Llandysul anglers made a second attempt at establishing an angling association, and they were able to lease eight miles of fishing between Henllan and Maesycrugiau. Permits for trout and sewin fishing cost 5s (25p, which was a lot in those days) and it cost just £2 for a season's salmon fishing. Yet again, through lack of local support and perhaps poor management, the association ceased to function two years later.

Fishing was a major contributor to the livelihood of John Lewis 'Pysgotwyr' (left) seen here with his colleague Mr Howells, a coachman who worked at The Porth Hotel. The fine brace of salmon in this picture came from the River Teifi *circa* 1920.

Fishing licences and club membership fees

Licence duties and club membership costs remained closely correlated. In 1930, the Teify and Ayron Fishery District licence duty for a rod and line for salmon fishing was £1-16s per year, £1 per month or 15s per fortnight. Note that the district fishery board used the old spelling of both the Teifi itself and of northerly neighbour, a river that we refer to today as the Aeron. Many other names have changed, too; indeed, at that time, Llandyssul had an extra *s* in its spelling at the time, and so it remained for some years, as you will see from the printing along the left-hand edge of the old licence, below. You can still see the old spelling of Llandyssul on some of the older road signs in and around the valley.

A Teify seine netting licence cost £6, which was just over three times the cost of a rod licence, while trout fishing licences cost 3s-6d (about 17p) per year or 2s (10p) per week. Those licence fees had not altered since 1922. Incidentally, at that time the angling season for salmon ran from 15th February to 16th October, while trout fishing was permitted between 1st March and 30th September.

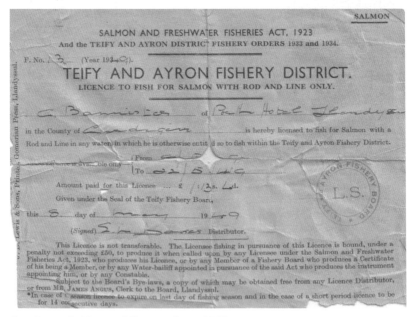

A salmon-fishing rod licence from 1949

I have no record of the charge per day for a room at The Porth Hotel in the 1930s, but I do know that their phone number was Llandysul 2. At that time the proprietor, D Davies, was advertising *'Five Miles of Salmon and Trout Fishing on the River Teify Preserved and free to visitors staying at the hotel'*. Today The Porth Hotel's telephone number is 01559 362202 – that final *2* has persisted down the decades.

John Still with a 56½ lb kelt found on the Teifi in about 1936. Caught on rod and line before spawning this might well have beaten the 64 lb British record salmon, from the Tay – a record that still stands today

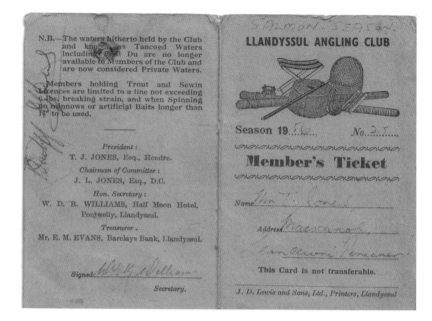

N.B.—The waters hitherto held by the Club and known as Tancoed Waters including Pwll Du are no longer available to Members of the Club and are now considered Private Waters.

Members holding Trout and Sewin Licences are limited to a line not exceeding 6 lbs. breaking strain, and when Spinning no minnows or artificial Baits longer than 1½" to be used.

President :
T. J. JONES, Esq., Hendre.

Chairman of Committee :
J. L. JONES, Esq., D.C.

Hon. Secretary :
W. D. R. WILLIAMS, Half Moon Hotel, Pontwelly, Llandyssul.

Treasurer .
Mr. E. M. EVANS, Barclays Bank, Llandyssul.

Signed.......................
Secretary.

SALMON SEASON

LLANDYSSUL ANGLING CLUB

Season 19.5.6., No..2.5....

Member's Ticket

Name.......................

Address.......................

This Card is not transferable.

J. D. Lewis and Sons, Ltd., Printers, Llandyssul

Rules.

1. A time limit of half an hour is allowed to any member fishing any pool, in the event of another member waiting to fish the same pool. [For Salmon].

2. Salmon Tickets : Season £5; Weekly £2/2/-; Trout and Sewin : Season £1/1/- ; Weekly 10/-.

3. All Tickets to be countersigned by the Financial Secretary. Ticket Register to be kept, and all members to sign same when obtaining Tickets.

4. Tickets are not transferable, and are to be produced when asked for by any member of the Club.

5. Ticket holders are particularly warned against doing any damage to growing crops, fences, or other property. They are also requested to close all gates, and not take their dogs on the lands.

6. Any person found fishing with illegal bait will forfeit his ticket, and automatically be debarred from further membership.

7. Any member convicted of an offence of the Fishing laws or infringe on the Rules of the Club shall be liable to forfeit his ticket.

8. All surplus money in the hands of the Club at the end of the season shall be utilised for the improvement of the Club's property.

9. The Club reserves full powers regarding the issuing of tickets—or otherwise.

10. Bottom fishing is disallowed between one hour after sunset and one hour before sunrise.

11. Tickets will be issued to school children at 5/- per Season.

12. Any person or persons found fishing on the Club's waters without tickets will be prosecuted.

13. It is the duty of every member to request any person found fishing to produce his ticket and on failure to do so, his name and address should be taken and reported to the Club Secretary.

14. All disputes shall be settled by the General Meeting, and their decision shall be accepted as final.

15. The Secretary shall call an Extraordinary General Meeting, on the application in writing from any five members.

16. The Chairman and Secretary have discretion to issue tickets or otherwise, and if in doubt to submit the application to the Club.

17. The Club reserve the right to alter or cancel any rule without notice.

18. Local Men or women serving in Her Majesty's Forces, or Merchant Navy, are allowed to fish the Club's Waters free of charge—as guests of the Club.

19. A ticket holder accepts the above rules as binding on himself.

20. As no Trout and Sewin Tickets will be issued to Salmon Board Licence holders, all persons must produce their Fishery Board Licence when taking out Club Membership Card.

21. The waters hitherto held by the Club and known as Tancoed Waters including Pwll Du are no longer available to Members of the Club and are now considered Private Waters.

Note.—In addition to this permit, the usual Board Licence must be held, obtainable at 4 Bridge St., Llandyssul.

Llandysul A A salmon permit (price £5) and rules for the season 1956

Formative years

During the immediate post-war years members of the armed services returned home to the Teifi Valley to find that the whole of the middle reaches were controlled by private syndicates and wealthy businessmen: it was practically impossible to get a day's fishing. This position remained unaltered until Llandysul was able to re-establish an angling association, through the kindness of local benefactor Mrs Douglas Fraser. After discussions with Artie Jones, the lady became so concerned at the plight of the local anglers that she offered her fishery, the Waunifor Estate Waters, at an annual lease of £90. Only after approving the choice of Chairman and Secretary, having first established their credentials, did Mrs Douglas Fraser agree to a deal; the club was officially established on 14th February 1949, and at the founding meeting the policy of the association was defined as:

- At all times to better the position of the local angler, and to encourage anglers from all walks of life to become members.
- When the opportunity arose, to purchase local fishing rights.
- To make association waters available to all visitors so as to encourage tourism.
- To accept any person, on payment of a season permit fee, as a full member.
- All surplus money in the hands of the Association at the end of any season would be utilised for the benefit of the association's property.
- Pensioners and schoolboys (trout fishing only) receive concessionary permits.

1957 Welsh International Team, including Artie Jones, at Loch Leven

At the inaugural meeting, it was unanimously agreed that the association should be a democratic one and that an annual general meeting would be held. An Executive Committee would manage the affairs of the association, and all officers and committee would be elected annually by private vote.

The association's first chairman was Mr J L Jones, with Mr Willy (Half Moon) Williams as the secretary. For the first season, the membership comprised 23 salmon anglers, who each paid £5 each, and 17 sewin and trout anglers whose fees were 10/- (50p) per season. In that first year the fishing was excellent, with one angler grassing 47 salmon. All 'clean fish' would have been killed in those days, of course.

Early fishing successes

It would be easy to concentrate on salmon and sea trout and forget that some wonderful trout fishing was also available on club waters. For example, on 17th July 1954, retired schoolmaster Willie Lloyd James landed a brown trout weighing 8lb. The monster wild trout was 28 inches long and 15 inches in girth. Scale readings showed it to be more than ten years old.

Willie Lloyd James with an 8 lb trout caught on the Teifi in 1954

Financial struggles

The early years were difficult financially. In November 1949 the club held its first annual general meeting. The financial balance was read out; it was a mere £5-1s-6d.

During the close season of 1949-50, the association managed to secure a lease on two more miles of fishing, increasing the total to four miles. By November 1950, at the second AGM, the profit for the year had risen to £45-5s, and a proposition was put forward to reduce the permit charges for the following year in view of this profit. This motion was defeated, but perhaps it was a warning to the committee of the young association to seek advance notice of such motions lest history should repeat itself and the association collapse due to insufficient funding, as had already happened twice in the past.

In 1951 the association accounts showed a credit balance of £104-15s-6d, but in the following season this balance reduced to £84-10s. Consequently, in order to improve the club's financial position an Entertainments Committee was formed with the object of raising funds through dances, raffles etc. The idea was to subsidise the association's members so as not to have to increase the subscriptions for the following season. It worked. By 1953 the association's account was in credit by £284. This was the pattern until 1963, by which time the bank balance stood at £884. Over fourteen years the average annual profit had been just £63 per year.

In 1960, the association sought to purchase its first fishing, known as the Tan-y-Coed Fishery (now owned by the club). This was an excellent two-mile stretch of fishing close to the village of Llandysul. Our initial bid of £7,000 was not acceptable to the vendor. We were given a second bite at the cherry and we increased our offer to £10,000 and then to £11,500, but we were reportedly out-bid by a private syndicate from Llanelli. The price they were reputed to have paid was £13,500. (We now believe from studying the deeds that the syndicate paid only £10,000. Had someone put pressure on the vendor not to sell to the association?)

The lower limit of the Tan-y-Coed fishing, which overlaps our Dol Watts fishery on the opposite bank.

On any rational analysis the association was not really in a position to buy Tan-y-Coed in 1960, having a bank balance of about £800 - insufficient to cover even the deposit. This purchase would have necessitated a ten-fold increase in permit prices in order to service the purchase price and bank charges, and at even the most optimistic projection it would have taken many years to repay the debt.

In 1957 the founding chairman, Mr J L Jones, died and Dr W D V Roderick from Llanelli was appointed in his place. Two years later, in January 1959, Lampeter Angling Association asked Llandysul A A to take them over, and at a specially convened General Meeting it was agreed to proceed with the merger.

The meandering Teifi at Lampeter

1963 was a landmark year for Llandysul Angling Association. At its AGM, in November, Artie Jones was appointed secretary. Seeking funding to purchase fisheries, Artie Jones approached the Sports Council for Wales but was told that funding angling clubs was not one of their objectives and that their grant-aid criteria did not permit them to do so. This Artie did not accept, and so he began a campaign of publicity to get the Sports Council criteria changed to include angling clubs and associations.

The newspapers took up the cause, as did the BBC. And it worked. The Sports Council accepted that angling clubs could in future apply for grant aid, and Llandusul A A was able to obtain financial assistance at a time when it was most needed.

Artie also campaigned for relief from local council rates; this put Llandysul A A in a better position when fisheries came on to the market. The first purchase was made in 1965, and many others followed during the next thirty years But perhaps his greatest triumph came in 1981, when he secured for the club 540yds of right-bank fishing at Llandysul, including a 13-acre smallholding known as Tyrdref. In this Artie and the committee saw potential benefits to the association and to the local community in general. Many will recognise the plot in question: it now provides excellent playing field facilities plus a waterside walk enjoyed by locals and visitors.

Support for young anglers

For several years, the late Trevor Hirons, a Welsh international flyfisher, gave lessons to youngsters on the River Teifi. Then, in 1986, Derek Hoskin and I began running courses in angling safety, water life, casting and flyfishing. In the course of the next sixteen years we taught more than 1000 young anglers, some of whom have gone on to become outstandingly able flyfishers. We also made a video film of the events of the course, and parents were invited to watch the video, in the Tysul Hall at Llandysul, at the end of the course. For the next two years, I ran the courses with my partner Sue Parker, and in 2004 Eric Davies and Peter Jones, both qualified angling coaches, extended the programme of tuition by running additional days of fishing throughout the summer holidays.

Steffan Jones and Jonathan Hoare are two of the many young anglers who attended these lessons and went on to become world class anglers, fishing for Wales in junior international matches.

It became a tradition that the winner of the casting competition would receive the Tom Howells Memorial Shield and a tackle prize, while there was also an award for sportsmanship based upon an initiative set up with generous donations from the late Cecil Thomas, a founder member of Llandysul Angling Association.

The late Cecil Thomas, who donated trophies and tackle so that a prize could be awarded annually to a young angler demonstrating great sportsmanship during the summer flyfishing lessons

Fortieth anniversary celebrations

In 1998, as the club was approaching its fortieth anniversary, I had an article published in Trout and Salmon magazine entitled *Teifi Celebrations*. In it *I said*:

'Summer visitors might be excused for thinking that the Teifi is a small river, but local folk know otherwise. Carrying more water to the sea in a year than Old Father Thames, the Teifi can rise very quickly and, sadly, has claimed the lives of many a careless wader over the years. During the autumn rains of 1987 the river rose nearly 20 feet in places, causing considerable devastation...'

Well, nowadays the weather seems to have become even more stormy and unpredictable, and nowadays the Teifi overflows its banks several times a year.

A day after the peak of the flooding, the arches of Llechryd Bridge are still not visible

The past two decades haves been a busy time for Llandysul A A. With the decline of spring salmon and a substantial increase in the numbers of sea trout reaching our Llanybydder and Lampeter fisheries during the summer, the pattern of fishing has changed a great deal. Autumn is now the time when most of our salmon are caught, while for the past few years the summer grilse run has been either very late or rather sparse. Surely by coincidence, 1988 was also a very good salmon season for our river, as elsewhere, but to date there is no evidence of sustained recovery. In 1998 grilse made a remarkable comeback - and not just on the River Teifi. And yet there remains hope: although 2004 will not go down as a vintage year for sea trout or for grilse, the Teifi total salmon catch figure, when published, could be exceptional.

Mr Alan Banister with a salmon caught on Horse Pool, Dolgrogws, in 1992

Dr Ian Thomas with a salmon of over 15 lb caught in 2004

The Artie Jones legacy

Much of the historical information presented above I gleaned from discussions with Artie Jones and from press cuttings and notes that he had collected over the years. Long-standing members will perhaps be aware of Artie's immense contribution to the development and success of this club. It even extends to fishing, as this extract from an article in *The Tivyside* newspaper shows. It was published in 1951 - a year before the Stanley Matthews Cup Final and the coronation of Her Majesty Queen Elizabeth II. The headline reads:

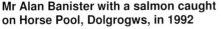

> **Llandysul Draper Welsh Champion**
> *Though formed only three years ago, the Llandysul Angling Club made a striking rise to fame over the weekend.*
> *At the end of the Welsh Fly Fishing Association championships, at the Claerwen Reservoir, on Saturday, their club had won the Luron Shield for the best team performance, having landed thirteen trout weighing 6lb 9oz, and one of their members, Mr Artie Jones, a 32-year old Llandysul draper, having become the Welsh champion fly fisherman, winning the Wynn Kirby Cup and a valuable fishing rod. The champion cup and shield are now on display in the Alma Sports Shop in Llandysul... ...and although Mr Jones is very modest about his success, he has certainly put Llandysul on the angling map.*

The Luron Shield

To the end, Artie continued to be modest about his achievements, but his record as an angling club secretary remains second to none. He was secretary of Llandysul A A for nearly 40 years. When he took over the helm the club had less than £1000 in the bank and owned no fishing whatsoever. As you read through the descriptions of our fisheries, you may have noticed that with but one exception they were all secured during Artie's period in office. Having worked with him on many of the more recent fishery purchases, I know just how stressful such negotiations can be.

Despite his own declining health and that of his wife, Megan, Artie Jones continued to strive to secure new waters for the club and to ensure that the fisheries we already own and control were and maintained for the benefit of members present and future. From my personal knowledge this can easily take fifteen hours a week when things are running smoothly and it becomes almost a full-time job whenever we have to deal with serious threats to the future of our fisheries.

In 1993, when Artie had been secretary for thirty years, a ceramic plaque, hand-painted with a kingfisher perched and looking over a river, was commissioned and fixed to the wall outside his home, Glas-y-Dorlan. It was a small thank you from the committee to the man who had steered the club through its fortieth anniversary. Now, fifteen years on, this book is another, albeit inadequate, tribute to a man who has done more than anyone I know for the future of club fishing in the Wales.

Famous Fishers of the Teifi

Famous for its salmon and trout fishing for well over a century, the River Teifi has long held a special place in game angling literature. Inevitably, it has attracted the attention of some illustrious visitors, including writers, broadcasters and many other well-known personalities from the worlds of sport, politics and entertainment.

Augustus Grimble

One hundred years ago, a man called Augustus Grimble wrote a series of books about the game fishing rivers of Ireland, of Scotland, and of England and Wales. *The Salmon and Sea Trout Rivers of England and Wales* first appeared as a limited edition of 350 copies in 2004. A second, revised and enlarged edition appeared in 1913 and remains a much-quoted reference book to this day.

Grimble has much praise for the Teifi as a salmon river. Strange as it may seem, however, sea trout get barely a mention - strange, that is, until you check through the catch results for the last twenty years of the nineteenth century. At that time, catching sea trout on the Teifi was almost unheard of.

What is clear is that sewin have been encroaching progressively into the upper reaches of the main river, and this may in part at least explain why the resident trout population has declined. So was agricultural pollution from pesticides already having an insidious effect forty or fifty years ago?

Bernard Venables

The most successful British writer of fishing books since Isaac Walton, Bernard Venables was a founder of *Angling Times* and of *Trout and Salmon* magazine. He was also the creator of the Daily Mirror's *Mr Crabtree* column, which was published in the early days of Llandysul Angling Association. His cartoon strip book Mr Crabtree Goes Fishing has sold well over two million copies.

Bernard first visited the Teifi in 1949, and he returned in 1996 as a guest of Llandysul Angling Association, fishing on our beats at Llandysul and Lampeter. Remarking on the scenery of the Teifi Valley, Bernard Venables described it as *'one of the most beautiful and unspoilt places he has ever visited'*. And that must be considered praise indeed from someone who was an internationally renowned artist and fisherman and had travelled the world and seen so many famous rivers.

The late Bernard Venables OBE fishing on the River Teifi

To mark Bernard's ninetieth birthday and his award of an OBE, Llandysul Angling Association made him an honorary member. He was a great joy to be with and such an inspiring fishing companion.

Oliver Kite

Older readers may remember the series of flyfishing programmes by writer and broadcaster Oliver Kite. In the 1960s, the River Teifi was *Kite's Country* in more than one sense: that was the name of the BBC series that major Oliver Kite made. It is also appropriate because the upper Teifi and Towy in particular were important strongholds of the red kite, a bird whose numbers plummeted to alarming scarcity in the first half of the twentieth century. Oliver Kite used to start his season with the March brown hatch, fishing for trout on the Teifi. His favourite imitative fly pattern, which he invariably used when Large Dark Olives were hatching, is known as *Kite's Imperial*. For those who might like to ties up some, the 'recipe' is as follows:

Hook	Up eyed sizes 14-18.
Thread	Purple
Tail	Honey dun (light ginger or sandy) cock hackle fibres
Body	Heron herl ribbed with fine wire
Hackle	Honey dun (light ginger or sandy) cock

Sadly, having achieved a life-long ambition to secure fishing of his own on the River Wylie, Oliver Kite suffered a premature death. Fortunately, the BBC has published a set of video films (black and white, of course) of *Kite's Country*.

President Jimmy Carter

We constantly try to convince politicians that flyfishing is no longer the preserve of medics, clerics and high profile public figures; however, there are some notable exceptions including former Prime Minister Alec Douglas Home. Looking across the pond the gentle art has provided relaxation for many high-ranking officials and politicians, but without doubt one of the most ardent of game anglers was and still is Jimmy Carter, 39th President of the United States of America, whose single term in the White House ran from 1977 until 1981. Six years later, Jimmy Carter visited Wales and fished the rivers Cothi and Teifi as well as Llyn Clywedog near Llanidloes. By all accounts he is no mean flyfisher.

It was to the River Teifi that former US president Jimmy Carter came when he had the opportunity to fish here in Wales. His host on that visit was Welsh flyfishing maestro Moc Morgan.
(Photo credit: pdimages.com)

Moc Morgan OBE

Moc Morgan has a special affinity with the Teifi, having lived for most of his life close to the river at Pontrhydfendigaid, in the upper reaches, where he was the headmaster of the local school. Moc, an honorary member of Llandysul A A, is author of the very successful book The Trout and Salmon Flies of Wales and co-author, with Dr Graeme Harris, of Successful Sea Trout Fishing. He is well known in Wales as a TV broadcaster and erstwhile secretary of the Welsh Salmon & Trout Association. Not at all surprisingly, Moc's son Hywel Morgan has become not merely a very good flyfisher but a world champion fly caster.

Here are the tying details for one of Moc Morgan's most famous sewin flies, the *Cert*. The name says it all!

Hook	Size 4 to 10 single or double
Silk	Black
Body (rear)	Flat silver tinsel
Body (front)	Black seal fur
Rib (front)	Flat silver tinsel
Hackle	Black cock
Wing	Black squirrel with green peacock sword
Cheeks	Jungle cock

HRH Charles, Prince of Wales

The Prince of Wales has a great passion for game angling. Needless to say, Prince Charles has fished the River Teifi and, by all accounts, shown great skill in doing so. The Teifi is known as The Queen of Spate Rivers, and so our links with the royal family are clearly established.

Her Majesty the Queen Mother also had an involvement with Llandysul A A. When, on behalf of the association, I wrote to her on matters of great concern to us that we believed might affect the future of game angling here on the River Teifi, she always replied without delay and provided a message of support and encouragement. Would that it had been possible to see the Queen Mother cast a line on the Queen of Rivers! But it was not to be.

Gareth Edwards

Having earned fame for life on the rugby field, Gareth Edwards might have been forgiven if he had chosen to rest on his laurels. He did not. Having worked as a company director in the water industry he still made time to hone his angling skills. Gareth is one of that remarkably small group of people who have fished Llandysul A A waters with our secretary Artie Jones. Artie hardly ever gets the opportunity to fish, but he made effort to go fishing with Gareth, and by all accounts they enjoyed some great sport on the Teifi.

Although Gareth Edwards has pursued many a quarry with rod and line, his particular passions are salmon and sewin - swift, powerful and difficult to deceive... entirely appropriate!

Martin James

A most entertaining and thought-provoking speaker, Martin James has on more than one occasion contributed to Llandysul A A's winter programme. For a quarter of a century Martin James has been a BBC broadcaster and a writer too. His published works include an autobiography and numerous magazine articles on fishing, wildlife and the countryside. Not only has Martin entertained us on winter evenings, but he has also acted as an ambassador of our club both in the UK and abroad. He makes many radio and TV programmes, not only in the UK but also in America and Canada, and the River Teifi and Llandysul A A have featured in several of these broadcasts. I have made many programmes with Martin over the past twenty years, and it is always a great pleasure to broadcast with such a true professional.

All too rarely does Martin James get a chance to visit the River Teifi Valley, but he is always ecstatic about its scenic beauty and the lovely wild brown trout of the Teifi that provide such a challenge to the dry fly fisher.

Writer and broadcaster Martin James

Martin suffers from multiple sclerosis, but whenever he is well enough (and sometimes when he is not) he likes to get out in all kinds of weather. He catches a lot of fish, killing none; he also continues to add to his extensive knowledge of wildlife and ecology, so that his campaigns on behalf of angling and conservation are based upon facts and scientific evidence. It's a lesson we all can learn.

George Melly

One of the great entertainers of our time, George Melly is also an art connoisseur of some renown, having written extensively and hosted radio and television programmes on the subject. But it is as a jazz singer that George is perhaps best known, and in this role he is held in high regard throughout the world. What may not be such common knowledge is that George Melly's other great love is flyfishing. Because of this, we were particularly pleased when George accepted our invitation to cast the first line on a new fishery we purchased in 1995.

George caught no sewin on his first night at our Castell Pyr fishing, but he demonstrated his expertise with the dry fly the following morning at Cwmmackwith. His secret, of course, is practice. He honed his skills on the River Usk, where for some years he owned a lovely stretch at his home just south of Brecon.

George Melly fishing at Castell Pyr, with unhelpful advice from me

With his keen eye for things of great beauty, it cam as no surprise when George described the Llandysul A A fisheries at Castell Pyr and Cwmmackwith as *"Quite magnificent"*. Thank you, George. Please visit us again soon.

Brian Clarke

The Times angling correspondent, author and broadcaster Brian Clarke visited the Teifi in March of 1996, giving us a memorable presentation on trout fishing tactics - based partly on the best-selling book *The Trout and The Fly*, which he co-authored with John Goddard.

With a sequence of colour slides, Brian explained how his approach to trout fishing had developed. Stealth and presentation were two of the key points that he stressed. Indeed, while the USD fly patterns (upside down tying on the hook, so that the point remains above the surface) were developed to cope with 'educated' trout, Brian Clarke admits that he rarely if ever uses them nowadays. He prefers simple tyings of the right general form, size and colour. An example is his polythene-winged spinner. He says that he now uses no other spinner imitation: this one simple pattern works as well as any and better than most. Here are the tying details:

Hook	Size 16
Tail	Ginger cock hackle fibres
Body	Equal mix of olive and brown seal fur plus a few fibres of hot orange
Wing	Polythene, cut from clear kitchen bag; tied flat (spent)
Hackle	None

The day after his talk, Brian Clarke and I set off in search of brown trout. The weather was terrible and March Browns refused to hatch. We saw just one trout rise. Needless to say Brian covered it with one of his close imitation dry flies and landed (and carefully returned to the river) a wild brown trout of a pound or so in weight.

Brian Clarke tackling up at Lampeter

Talking with Brian at the launch, in 1998, of our fishing-in-wales.com website, I was pleased to hear that he, too, had found his visit to the Teifi memorable. I do hope he will come back soon to try for a Teifi sea trout. Meanwhile, keep in touch with Brian Clarke via his column in The Times on the first Monday of every month.

Peter O'Reilly

No one has done more for Ireland's angling tourism industry than that doyen of Irish game fishing, Peter O'Reilly. Peter kindly paid us a visit in the autumn of 1996, when we arranged for him to give a talk in St Peter's Hall, Carmarthen. To a large audience - bigger than at any other UK venue during his visit - he gave an enthralling presentation covering many aspects of salmon and trout fishing.

Irish game angling supremo Peter O'Reilly

Peter, an enthusiastic proponent of habitat improvement as a means of restoring fisheries to their former glory, explained how Lough Sheelin's wild trout stocks had been increased by 400 per cent by reducing the pig-farm pollution and restoring small breeder streams to full productivity. He also practises catch-and-release of wild brown trout - the glorious River Boyne runs close to his home in Navan.

Peter O'Reilly's books about the rivers, lakes and fishing flies of Ireland are essential reading for anyone contemplating a fishing trip to the Emerald Isle.

Orri Vigfusson

It is largely due to the vision and initiative of Icelander Orri Vigfusson that the high-seas nets off Greenland and Faroes have been curtailed. Orri is vice chairman of the North Atlantic Salmon Fund, working to conserve salmon stocks in the North Atlantic by buying out salmon netting rights in high-seas fisheries.

Orri Vigfusson during his 1998 visit

Funds are raised by voluntary contributions from anglers in salmon-fishing countries bordering the Atlantic, and commercial netsmen are paid to relinquish their rights to fish for salmon. This initiative is particularly valuable in protecting the large multi-sea-winter salmon that feed far from their natal rivers.

Orri was the guest of Llandysul A A in 1996, when he made a presentation in Carmarthen to the anglers of West Wales. He is in regular correspondence with Llandysul A A, and by the end of the 1998 season the club had already made contributions of over £3000 to the North Atlantic Salmon Fund. (Members voted at their annual general meeting in 1995 to donate £1 per full member plus £1 per visitor permit to the Fund.)

Despite visiting us on more than one occasion, Orri has yet to cast a line on the River Teifi - a situation we hope to rectify soon.

Charles Jardine

Charles Jardine, with Melvin Grey, awarding a certificate to one of our Young Conservationists

Writing in Trout and Salmon in July 1997, Charles Jardine referred to the River Teifi as a river that *"...changes its form with almost every twist and turn of its journey to the sea."* Charles has a special relationship with the Teifi, and in 1995 he visited Llandysul Angling Association to give a talk to members and guests of the club. It was a memorable evening, and our only regret is that because of his many other teaching, painting and writing commitments Charles has so few opportunities to visit our club waters.

Charles Jardine and his family spent a day on our conservation project in August 1998, when more than two-dozen youngsters benefited from his extensive knowledge of entomology and water life. Naturally Charles, who is an honorary member of Llandysul A A, has an open invitation to visit our club waters.

Absent friends

Starting this section was very easy. Deciding where to stop is much more difficult. I must draw a line somewhere, and yet I have omitted so many well-known visitors including Jon Beer, Joe Chappel, Nick Hancock, John Horsey, Lord Moran, Steve Parton, David Shaw, Ken Wheelan, John Wilshaw and many others. It goes to show just how well off Llandysul A A is for friends. This is, nevertheless, an appropriate place to *say "Thank you, and do please visit us again soon"* to the many friends who have fished our waters during Llandysul A A's first fifty-six years.

The Whether Forecast

Whether there is a future for Angling depends – and of this I am quite convinced – more on the actions of anglers than of antis. Some of our opponents present a persuasive case for abolishing angling, but the great benefits of retaining our sport are not always voiced as clearly. It must be made quite clear why the natural water environment needs three million pairs of eyes providing early warning of pollution and other threats to wildlife and public health. We must also make sure that the general public is aware of what we contribute to habitat protection and wildlife conservation, and what would be lost if our sport were to be outlawed as, it seems, Hunting is destined to be. Abolition is a threat that we have to take seriously.

Throughout the history of Llandysul A A we have had to face up to one threat after another to the future of sport on the Teifi. In the 1970s ulcerative dermal necrosis (UDN), a terrible disease, threatened to wipe out the salmon of the Teifi and other British rivers. Despite virtually no opportunity to fish for salmon, members - and indeed the landowners from whom we were renting much of our fishing - remained loyal to the club, and so the club survived. The river improved, and we must continue working to secure further improvements.

When we have had to come to terms with the need to limit our catches, we have done so voluntarily, introducing bag limits and other conservation measures. For example members are not permitted to fish closer than fifteen yards apart, and this limits exploitation at hot spots; there is no spinning after sunset; and it is prohibited under our rules for any member to sell fish which have been caught on club waters. These and several other measures we have taken to conserve fish stocks. And most significantly, as we have added new waters to our portfolio of fishing opportunities, we have not increased the maximum number of members allowed under our constitution; in this way we have reduced by thirty per cent the number of anglers per mile who can fish our waters.

A Teifi salmon caught by Dr Ian Thomas in 1988

Despite all of these voluntary measures, pressure on salmon stocks continued, and in 1994 the National Rivers Authority, in reviewing the rod and net fishing byelaws for the Teifi, felt it necessary to propose further restrictions to limit exploitation of salmon on the Teifi and other Welsh rivers. Their preferred option was method restriction (fly only) to allow more salmon to escape capture and to spawn. The club's official response to the proposals was broadly supportive, although we lobbied hard for a substantial reduction in netting, highlighting the conservation byelaws brought in by our association. Other angling clubs in West Wales pressed for a shorter season with all methods permitted, and that is what was introduced in 1997. We pressed for, and secured, the agreement of the regulators (now The Environment Agency) to review the byelaws within five years, but continuing declines in salmon stocks have meant further restrictions on salmon fishing in spring, with mandatory release of all fish caught before 16th June. (The multi-sea-winter salmon tend to enter rivers early in the year, and these restrictions are intended to help that most seriously depleted component of the salmon run.)

The net limit on the estuary was reduced from six to four - the actual number of nets fishing immediately before the Net Limitation Order review. Because the netsmen objected, a costly Public Inquiry had to be held, and although the inspector upheld the NRA proposals the net restrictions were delayed by a year.

As I write this, the final chapter of this present book, the future of the Teifi fisheries is once more under review, with the net limitation orders again coming under the microscope. What is the fair allocation of fish between rods and nets? Should it be determined by considering the socio-economic benefits of each sector, as was recommended to Government in the final report of the recent *Salmon and Freshwater Fisheries Review*? And how do we assess the heritage value of the coracle fisheries?

One thing is very clear to me: until we can do something to cut dramatically the mortality of salmon at sea, the only fishing in rivers that has a sustainable future is fishing that has minimal impact on the survival and spawning prospects of those precious few salmon that succeed in making it back to our river.

Adopting new technologies

In another initiative, by contributing £3 per member to a fund for the operation of a fish counter on the Teifi, we were able to influence the decision of the Environment Agency to purchase and install a hydro-acoustic counter on the Teifi. This is now operational and enables fisheries scientists, when preparing future byelaw proposals, to take into account the out-of-season run of salmon which many believe may represent a significant proportion of the total salmon run on the Teifi, particularly in those years when the weather is dry and the river remains low in autumn. The results are published retrospectively, many months in arrears; this is largely because the raw data from the counter have to be batch processed to extract meaningful information about fish numbers, and despite the power of modern computers this, we are assured, takes a very long time.

We publicise Llandysul A A and the Teifi Valley extensively in articles, radio and television broadcasts and via the Internet, because we are proud of the club, proud of its culture and proud of its achievements. Even so we don't find it easy to maintain a full membership as, inevitably, each year some members hang up their rods through infirmity, or they move away or die. Recruiting new members is essential, however; only then can we raise the income necessary to fund all of the other initiatives, including maintenance work and new fishery purchases, that are essential to our vision for the future of the club. Adopting new technologies early is a principle that has serves Llandysul A A well. That is why, in 1997, we built our own website, which has been accessed more than ten million times so far, and provided a window into the Teifi Valley for people from all over the world.

Our interactive CD-ROM is the latest technology-based initiative designed to help our members and visitors learn more about the fishing we have to offer as well as the many other attractions in and around the Teifi Valley – including, of cours,e its outstanding scenic beauty and wealth of wildlife.

A culture of friendship and generosity

It is through the loyalty and commitment of its members that Llandysul Angling Association will either stand or fall. Our present position is essentially the result of people who have unselfishly shared their knowledge and passed on their skills and enthusiasm, affording a warm welcome and forging new friendships with visitors to our club and our community. That, as much as anything, has been for me the joy of chairing Llandysul Angling Association over the past eighteen years. The baton is now passing to a new chairman who will, I am sure, lead the club to a new future still firmly founded on the culture of friendship and generosity that has always been the hallmark of this association. And may it remain so as long as there are fish to swim in the River Teifi and anglers keen to cast for them.

Index